Executive Development Journeys

Executive Development Journeys

The Essence of Customized Programs

Cora Lynn Heimer Rathbone

Director of Executive Education,
Aston Business School

Featuring customized interventions at six leading corporates, collectively representing 280 interventions between 2002 and 2009, each ranging from one to 12 days, the norm being modular, of five days duration, resulting in an average of 40 weeks of delivery programs in each of seven years and over 10,000 face-to-face participant contact hours.

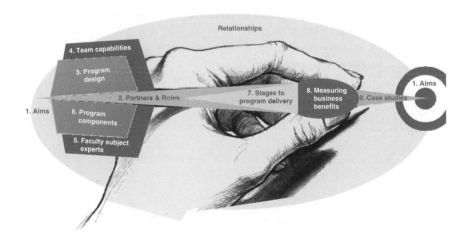

palgrave
macmillan

First published 2010 by
PALGRAVE MACMILLAN

Palgrave Macmillan in the UK is an imprint of Macmillan Publishers Limited, registered in England, company number 785998, of Houndmills, Basingstoke, Hampshire RG21 6XS.

Palgrave Macmillan in the US is a division of St Martin's Press LLC, 175 Fifth Avenue, New York, NY 10010.

Palgrave Macmillan is the global academic imprint of the above companies and has companies and representatives throughout the world.

Palgrave® and Macmillan® are registered trademarks in the United States, the United Kingdom, Europe and other countries.

ISBN 978–0–230–27481–5

This book is printed on paper suitable for recycling and made from fully managed and sustained forest sources. Logging, pulping and manufacturing processes are expected to conform to the environmental regulations of the country of origin.

A catalogue record for this book is available from the British Library.

A catalog record for this book is available from the Library of Congress.

10 9 8 7 6 5 4 3 2 1
19 18 17 16 15 14 13 12 11 10

Printed and bound in Great Britain by
CPI Antony Rowe, Chippenham and Eastbourne

To Jim and Alexa-Maria:
for keeping me real with questions such as
"And how will that help me be more effective in the real world?"

CONTENTS

ACKNOWLEDGEMENTS

Without the partnership of corporate clients, especially those named as "The Cast" and whose case studies appear as the final chapter of this book, this "journey" of executive development could not have been as informative. Nor would this synopsis of the essence of customized executive development programs exist. To those corporates, I am personally indebted. As each corporate is a collection of unique individuals, I am particularly thankful to those within them, at many levels, with whom I have worked hand-in-glove to design, constantly refine, populate, in some cases co-deliver and evaluate unique interventions. It has been an incredible honor to work with them.

Simultaneously, this seven-year "journey" would not have materialized without the faculty who co-labored with me. Together we created, structured, chiseled and delivered these interventions. From them emerged the prime inputs, including many creative exercises to exemplify their subjects. The quotes interspersed through the chapters, from some of the many who contributed richly, reflect voices of reason, of passion for their subject and of commitment to executive development.[1] Without exception, they have been indispensable partners in the work of transformational executive development.

Finally, without the skill of a flexible support team that project-managed all logistics and event-related issues, the volume undertaken would not have been possible, the quality of programs delivered would not have been assured.

To all three parties, eternal thanks!

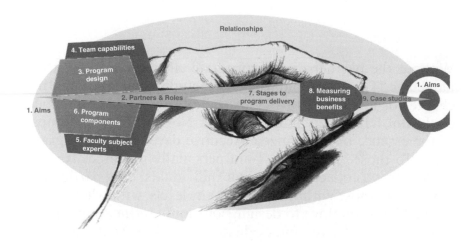

Investment in executive development has grown exponentially over the last few years. In particular customized programs, made to deliver to the precise needs of corporates, organizations and companies, have increasingly featured in business school remits.[1]

Amazingly, through the worst global recession since World War II (2008–2009), the commissioning of new tailor-made programs and the delivery of existing customized interventions continues nearly unabated.

Let's start at the very beginning. *Why* do successful corporates with their highly educated employees look to business schools for such development interventions? What are their aims in this, and therefore what kind of programs do they commission? What do those programs contain? Who are the principal contributors, and what attracts key faculty and subject experts to play a part? How can one measure the impact of such interventions?

Like a dart in the hand of a world-class player is a customized program in the hands of a dedicated delivery team. As with a dart, a customized program should be weighty and straight. As with a dart, whose efficacy lies in the craftsmanship of the shaft, so with a customized intervention, success lies in the relationships and clarity of roles of the core partners. As with a dart, whose balance depends on the feathers that also give it direction, so with a made-to-measure program, effectiveness arises from the balance and direction gained through the design process.

Clearly, the foundation of a customized program's quality depends on preparation, summarized in the up-front design. Notice to this end how packed to the left of the picture is the drawn "customized" dart. Yet without passionate and energetic delivery, both the dart and the customized program, however well designed, are ineffectual.

Like a dart, even the most refined customized intervention relies heavily on the human touch, that in-the-moment controlled, passionate throw (alias: delivery). Like a dart, a customized program needs expert handling, through which alone it has every chance of hitting the bulls-eye – again, and again, and again. Sustainably.

Analogy apart, what do these programs contain? What do they actually look like?

This brief synopsis addresses the above questions. It is written by a program director of customized interventions after seven years of practice at one of the world's leading business-school providers of customized programs. It summarizes the three prime reasons why customized programs are commissioned and enumerates the key aspects of successful interventions. With views from corporate sponsors, participants and faculty contributors, it gives a flavor of this breed of executive education through mini case studies of customized programs commissioned by six corporates.

Its purpose is to inform HR and talent development communities, and to structure the thinking of those who commission and design executive development interventions. The aim is to better ensure that such interventions are indeed transformational, skill enhancing for global executives and able to generate business benefit for the corporates within which their organizers have the responsibility and privilege of working.

Why do *major corporates* engage business schools to develop their executive and talent populations?

After all, the most significant corporates recruit the best people from the best academic institutions in the first place. Established organizations integrate recruits through a series of social and structured activities that introduce new starters to the technical requirements of the job they have been taken on to do and to the culture or way of working within the corporate. Beyond the young intakes, a well-connected industry of head-hunters has emerged that connects the most appropriate individuals to corporates that seek to fill specific and often senior positions. The recruits, once integrated into the new corporate, are presumably suitably skilled for their task.

Clearly, most major corporates know how to attract and select the individuals whose technical and personal skills will add most value to their organizations. It follows that these people choices are made to satisfy both the short and long-term operational and strategic needs of the entity. Thus, having their human capital in place, are these corporates not best placed to develop their own talent?

Anecdotally, a symbiotic connection exists between the continuous self-ignited development of key players, which in itself creates organizational growth, and the organizational challenges that provoke and elicit the development of the best. Thus, successful companies emerge through the ingenuity and self re-creative ability of their talent. Simultaneously, their talent grow through the challenges they master and the new realities they engender.

Beyond "natural" and organizationally "nurtured" develop-mental activities, existing executives arguably make the best "developers" of others within and beyond their corporates. In this vein, references to "mentors" and "coaches" pepper both organizational conversations and "management" literature. Who better to learn from than those who have succeeded in the given environment?

So why do corporates turn to *business schools* for the development of their very highly rated individuals and teams? And what do those development programs look and feel like? What broadly do they deliver?

One answer to the first question could be that, as evidence suggests, young talent seek to join companies that will invest in their formal development. To be an "employer of choice", corporates will increasingly be pressured to tangibly develop the talent they wish to attract and retain.

The contribution from business-school-provided customized programs serves this demand and is complementary to that provided by the corporate – the induction programs, on-the-job projects or development opportunities and executive sessions. Customized programs cannot replace the development that is provided by the organization. They can however serve several useful purposes that in-house interventions would struggle to satisfy.

This brief synopsis of seven years at one of the world's leading business schools serves to identify:

- The three main aims that drive corporates to commission customized interventions.[1] In general, quoting one senior executive: "Made-to-measure programs enable us to design development opportunities for critical populations that address very clear sets of needs aligned to our strategic objectives. Delivering such programs within a contained time frame ensures we get a critical mass of talent thinking differently, aligned to our strategic intent. That makes for a very compelling proposition."[2]
- The triad of core partners whose joint forces, from design to delivery, give birth to customized programs. What roles does each fulfill? What is the basis of the relationships and the trust that must underpin successful customized interventions?

- The fundamental aspects and techniques in the design of customized programs. How can you canvas widely the thoughts of many within the organization? How do you hard-wire effective processes for learning together with relevant program content into tightly timed designs?
- The capabilities required of a delivery team. Rarely is a customized program a "one-person" show. Highly educated, rightly demanding, experienced and time-poor program participants can only be satisfied by a spectrum of individuals working as a mutually supporting collective. So who are the core team members and what capabilities must they bring to the party?
- Proven keys to engaging faculty and subject experts whose contribution is central to successful interventions. How do you engage the passionate participation of effective yet notoriously independent subject experts? As one business school dean put it: "Gathering faculty is like herding cats." A second proffered: "Faculty are connected – through the central heating system."
- Program elements that make the development journey a living experience, accepting that key subjects are necessary but not sufficient for success. A selection of 22 program components are considered, a handful of which must be included for the program to be useful to participants and applicable in the context of the corporate.
- A sequential process to be followed. Seven steps along a pathway of relationships should be followed to bring a program into existence. From winning the business to measuring business benefits, always underpinned by client management, the disciplines of made-to-measure program development are clear.
- Processes through which to identify business benefits derived from development programs. Considered are a number of principles and mechanisms for measuring the business benefit of executive interventions. Tackled directly is the challenge and need to isolate benefits derived uniquely from the program, given the context of continuous change within which our corporates operate.
- Reality – seen through the examples of real development journeys commissioned by six fabulous corporates and travel companions.

1. SMG – Stewart Milne Group

A major regional player

THE UK leader in timber construction; a program suite for five layers of management that ran from December 2003 to May 2005

*Equipping all man-managers and leaders to reach their potential – to **be more strategic, better people managers and greater deliverers of competitive quality.***

2. BNFL/BNG/Sellafield

A major national player

THE world's most concentrated nuclear site; a series of inter-connected programs that have run continuously from 2003 to 2009

*Developing **commercial innovation leadership and accountable management** amongst executives, senior and middle managers in the midst of large-scale transformation*

3. France Telecom Orange

A major multinational player

THE innovative, fully integrated communication operator; continuous program run from 2004 to 2009

*A dynamic program for the **development of intrapreneurship***

4. EDF

A multinational technological leader

THE fifth largest global nuclear electricity producer; a four-program suite that has run continuously from 2004 to 2009

Designing and delivering executive development under the umbrella of the Corporate University to **accelerate business transformation**

5. L'Oréal

A global market leader

THE global leader in beauty products; three separate programs for progressively higher seniority, the first with continuous delivery from 2005 to 2009

TAM: Transition to advanced management

Enabling managers to make the **transition into heads of functions and members of management committees**

CMS: Country manager seminar

Enabling senior directors to **transition into the role of country managers (MDs)**

SCA: Strategic change architects

Equipping human resource directors to be **strategic change architects**

6. Oracle

A global giant

THE global information company; program run from 2007 to 2009

Supporting Oracle's key talents to become active **drivers of strategy and agents of change within their teams**

CHAPTER 1

Program aims

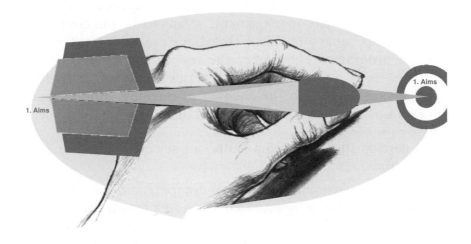

"Il faut cultiver notre jardin" (*Candide*, Voltaire)

Though they differ from corporate to corporate and are at the best of times connected to the strategy of the organization, some generic aims are often present. These aims fall into three dominant categories:

1. To **improve** the "**economic performance**" of the organization.

   These programs aim to improve a population's ability to enhance sales, reduce operating costs, tighten working capital, lower external charges (including taxes), and/or reduce the capital intensity of operations. Though they can be "functionally biased" and "siloed", in many ways these are business school "bread and butter" programs. They fit well within a business school's capabilities and often call upon the knowledge pools that feed MBA and EMBA programs.

In some cases, these programs allow business schools to draw from the emerging thinking of research clubs and PhD outputs.

2. To **enhance** the "**strategic thinking**" of key players towards the top or through the hierarchy of the organization.

Such programs tend to be transversal, to cut across business disciplines. They present a collage of subjects such as economics, strategy, finance, marketing, supply chain, operations and project management, wrapped in the context of leadership behaviors. Clear storylines are important within these programs. They carry the red thread of what could otherwise be a poorly connected series of independent albeit important topics. To the chagrin of business schools, such programs are occasionally referred to as "mini-MBAs".

3. To **develop** the "**leadership skills**" of selected talent or high potentials.

Beginning often with behavioral competencies or data from 360°s/performance appraisals, these programs can be the most creative of those delivered. Arguably, their design logic needs to be the clearest of all. More than with "strategic" programs and much more than with "economic performance" programs, the effectiveness of leadership programs depends on the social context created within the session itself.

Leadership doesn't exist in a vacuum. Leadership skills manifest in the context of others, with "appropriate" behavior being a function of many factors (e.g. organizational situations, industry, environment). Each cohort of participants therefore presents a perfect opportunity for sense-making, given the culture and situation of the company.

For leadership development programs to be effective, an environment must be created where participants are willing to honestly and personally look at themselves and their own behaviors. Only in so doing will they appropriate the concepts explored during the sessions. Contradictorily, participants need to be impacted by new incisive knowledge about themselves and *at the same time* feel that they are in a safe place, not under judgment, free to acknowledge and explore what are often uncomfortable novelties.[1] They need to think out of the box about themselves, and about themselves relative to significant others.

Naturally, the above three categories interface with each other. Often the difference is subtle. It is therefore very important to be clear about the emphasis of purpose, so that faculty can gear their material to achieve the deliverables that the corporate intends.

The emphasis on taught "tools, models or frameworks" within programs decreases progressively as you move counter-clockwise in the figure below from those that focus on "economic performance" to those that focus on "strategic thinking", with those that revolve around "leadership skills" being least reliant on the "how to" nature of tools. One manifestation of this is that the stronger the focus on "economic performance", the more concrete the sessions become and the more structured the learning can be.

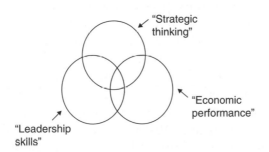

As a consequence, whereas the application of "taught" program elements from "economic performance" programs is relatively easy to track,[2] that from the strategy programs is harder to assess. Application of learning from the leadership sessions is hardest of all to measure. In part this results from the more indefinable nature of "strategy" and "leadership" as concepts and topics.[3]

Appropriate application of strategic and leadership concepts is more dependent on situations than is the case with tools that drive "economic performance". Things "strategic" and "behavioral" are much more "relative" than things aligned to "economic performance". Application is more subtle. Cause and effect are less directly coupled.

Though models exist that can form the backbone to strategic and leadership programs, these models only serve to frame new and emerging thinking from which the true value of such programs is derived. Clearly, the increased complexity of these subjects, and the interdependence of the same with often innumerable factors, influence the direct measurability or impact from such programs.

How do these different aims concretely affect the look and feel of a customized program? Let's draw from the programs of the six named corporates.

An example of a customized program that emphasized "economic performance" is the EDF suite. Though its four programs include one on "Strategy" and another on "People", the purpose of the suite is to accelerate the transformation of the EDF Group from a state-owned monopoly to a multinational commercial utility operating competitively in all of its regions. The storyline across the suite is one of "understand your market so that, within it, you can position EDF's strategy, strategize within your own business unit and lead your people to increasingly impressive performance". Packed with tools, the program aims to give participants an outside–in look at EDF and the energy market.[4] With those tools, applied in small breakout sessions, participants analyze, present and discuss their shared reality. The case study is EDF as presented by the participants themselves, coming from their very diverse group entities. As development partners, we do not instruct them in what they should do; we provide frameworks that provoke discussion, enabling participants to think differently.

During the period in which these programs have run, unrelated and separate from the programs themselves, the EDF Group implemented several efficiency campaigns in its different subsidiaries. With names like "Top Fit" in Germany and "Altitude €7,500M" in France, the Group drove permanent/sustainable, hitherto counter-cultural cost reductions in environments that had not previously experienced such activity. Tensions sometimes manifested in the customized programs themselves as messages from the sessions dovetailed, uncomfortably for some, with the cost-cutting activity within the business units.

Another example of a program whose primary focus was the enhancement of "economic performance" was Stewart Milne Group's customized suite. Facing its two major growth-limiting factors of labor and land shortages, the Group embarked on a program that would raise employees' awareness of how they could be more productive and drive greater perceived customer value whilst delivering to higher, more consistent quality standards. By subtitling the program "Reaching Your Potential", they subtly rooted the end-goal in the participants' authentic ability to deliver more. The fact that the program started with the facilitated development of the Group's first strategic plan ensured that the program purpose was to empower participants to achieve that newly defined enhanced performance.[5]

By contrast, examples of customized programs that emphasize the development of "strategic thinking" are those designed for BNFL/ Sellafield. Even within the middle management program, the aim is to enable participants to better lead by developing a broader view of their nuclear reprocessing and clean-up challenges.[6] As scientists and guardians of the world's most concentrated and complex nuclear storage sites, their backgrounds drive them to the detail, their thinking anchors them to the buildings/silos that they manage within the perimeter of their site. Yet with the new remit to operate these sites as commercial entities, the entire management team needed to adopt a helicopter view of the site as a whole within its unique ecosystem – in addition to, not in place of, the detail. All needed to clearly relate, in relevant and appropriate ways, to the interconnected and interdependent aspects of the site, to very significant external stakeholders, and to the larger "market" of nuclear reprocessing and nuclear waste management within which they exist as a major player.

A second program whose emphasis is on "strategic thinking" is that for France Telecom Orange. Tasked to raise the entrepreneurial spirit amongst the rank and file of promising managers and first-line directors, the program was designed to explore a business project as an entire entity. From the creation of a team, to the analysis of the market, to the definition of the unique proposition and detailing of the strategic plan for the commercialization of an innovative product or service, the program creates an environment and provides the tools with which participant teams can, from scratch, craft and present a holistic strategic plan. Often for the first time in their professional lives, they need to rise above their functional discipline, think beyond their business unit boundaries, extend well beyond the normal annual and quarterly business cycle to plan the launch of a new market offering.

A third "strategic thinking" program is that for L'Oréal's HR community: Strategic Change Architects. The purpose of this is to equip senior HR directors with the tools and a process for managing change in a strategic manner. L'Oréal wanted its HR directors not only to be strong change management experts but also, as strategic business partners, to guide general managers and business leaders to think about the wider implications of and possible alternatives to the changes they propose.

Moving to the third category of generic program aims, our corporate cast presents three examples of customized programs that are principally focused on the development of "leadership skills": Oracle's 4Sight, and L'Oréal's Transition to Advanced Management (TAM) and Country Manager Seminar (CMS).

The Oracle 4Sight program was created to support Oracle EMEA in the development of its future leaders. Successful, competitive and determined, participants bring their significant experience, knowledge of the market and unquestionable drive to the debates.[7] Key questions guide the program's three modules:

- How can/does Oracle continue to lead the industry?
- How can participants lead within Oracle to increase effectiveness across regions and lines of business?
- How can participants personally and authentically inspire higher levels of performance within their teams and through their client relationships?

Though this program is packed with tools, it is about how those tools enable participants to lead in their different contexts – as collaborators, as peers and as leaders.

TAM and CMS programs are part of L'Oréal's "Transition to ..." series.

TAM was designed in recognition of the fact that being an expert in a function and able to manage others within that expertise does not enable participants, all of whom are in their first functional directorship, to manage people who are themselves managers of others. Nor does it make them as individuals positive contributors to the management committees of which they as directors are now members. To manage beyond the realms of expertise requires a new basis for confidence and a new source for contribution. Behavior and self-awareness within that becomes a focal point for credibility. The program is built to maximize self-discovery, supported by strong, evidence-based feedback and coaching from executive coaches, facilitators and fellow participants as peers. Only two frameworks feature in the week. Both serve to help participants benchmark themselves in their leadership journey against the L'Oréal competencies at their level of the organization.

Two seniority levels higher, CMS is structured to equip country managers to lead across the whole of L'Oréal's business divisions within a country. Leadership at this level is truly lonely, especially for those whose countries are quite distant from the corporate seat at Clichy near Paris, France. The program unpacks leadership frameworks in three contexts:

- for growing the business
- for creating a great place in which people can work, and
- for being a responsible corporate citizen, given the country context.

In the safety of small numbers, participants explore for themselves what it means to individually be the personification of this very organic, uniquely oral culture that is L'Oréal – in the country they manage – and conversely represent their country within L'Oréal HQ. Only thus will the country MDs be able to effectively grow the business, credibly create a great working environment, and responsibly manage the greater context.

Again, as most of the examples show, whilst the logic of the three categories of generic aims holds, programs frequently combine elements of all three purposes. The key question for the design and delivery partner is to ensure that the *emphasis* is correct and the exercises are appropriate, that all elements of the program are brought back to inform the "dominant logic" when answering the "so what" of the learning.

Even with clarity about the general aim of a program, design must be based on deep and extensive conversations with significant players within the organization. These include not only the internal commissioning team but also representatives from the population the program will serve, the bosses of possible participants, direct reports to those possible participants, and the senior executives whose strategies will be served by the up-skilled participants who emerge from the programs. To this end, key questions, aligned respectively to each of the three categories listed above, will be:

1. What new level of performance do you want individuals to be able to deliver?
2. What new conversations do you want individuals to provoke, with which they are not currently engaging?
3. What behaviors do you want to see in individuals that is different from the way in which they currently conduct themselves?

CHAPTER 2

Partners and roles

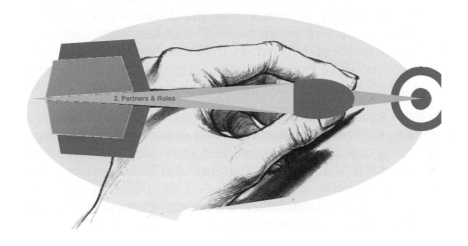

"Many hands make light work" (anon)

Whatever the aim of the intervention, however simple or complex it appears to be, fulfillment in the context of executive development requires partnership. Always this **partnership is tripartite: the client organization, the delivering faculty** and **the executive development team** who, as impresarios, stage these unique "productions".

Given that the "**client organization**" presents not only as the commissioning party within the organization but also and **principally** as the **participants upon arrival**, each time a program runs it is like the opening night of a new production. All the experience brought by the delivering cast must be humbly submitted to the expectations and fears of the participants – as individuals and within the dynamic of the groups that form, in parts and as a whole. Capturing these nuances in the first one to five minutes of participants' arrival is crucial to the success of each session, to the value that the program will add.

Complicating this complex and very human situation, some programs are created in **partnership with other business schools**, with the **delivery team** being a **composite** from both schools. Almost always these are at the request of the client organization. Competition and the desire to excel, to win the heart of the client organization and to promote one business school above another, can get in the way of cohesive program delivery. It certainly challenges delivery of programs as a seamless whole, and lasts throughout the life of the program. It is incumbent upon partnering business schools to build not only cooperative,[1] not even only coordinated[2] but ultimately collaborative relationships.[3]

Though obviously testing, organizations that are increasingly having to partner with other entities (e.g. across global blocs) in order to serve increasingly networked and composite clients seek to work with business schools that model effective collaboration within co-opetitive environments.[4] This trend is likely to increase. Collaborations between business schools may become a competitive advantage for those who can and do.

Through all discussions and considerations, the client must remain at the center. Particularly within the context of a consortium delivery team, it would be fraudulent to accept a commission for which you couldn't **agree** on the best and most appropriately skilled and sincerely motivated faculty cast. It would also be incompetent if you could not **challenge** alternative delivery configurations during the design process. This inevitably leads to tough conversations. Add to this the fact that clients sometimes demand what at first seems impossible. And scope often creeps to the point of endangering the program's desired results. That which must serve as the litmus test for each executive development intervention is the client organization's development needs, embodied within the participants' expectations for their personal development.

Let's unpack the role of each partner:

- The client organization is the purveyor of:
  - the culture of the organization
  - development needs relative to the strategy

- connection to career and talent managers with access to succession plans
- history of development activity within the corporate
- internal support structures to drive learning before, during and after the program
- an internal network for speakers, program mentors and participants
- the selection process from which emerges the final participant list
- "acceptability" of program design.

• Delivery faculty (including program director and corporate speakers):
  - are subject-matter experts: of existing knowledge pools, of new research or of practice-based thinking
  - are experts in learning processes
  - can have industry-specific knowledge, benchmarking understanding of the client organization
  - must possess strong teaching skills, knowing how best to impart knowledge, build experience, develop skills in participants
  - need strong facilitation skills to bring out and work with the knowledge of participants
  - should have breadth of cross-industry knowledge of their subject, not be boxed into one industry for the application of that subject
  - are authoritative and, to a large extent, impartial
  - have a degree of design strength – ability to conceptualize
  - have a passion for engaging with others, what some might label as "client management" skills.

• Executive development teams must include:
  - project and event managers
  - logistics organizers and administrators
  - "publishing" experts, to produce hard copy, web-sites, e-learning packages and learning portals
  - learning service providers, to administrate psychometric tools and to conduct assessment and development centers.

All three partners must **bring** these **unique contributions** to all phases of the program's duration.

CHAPTER 3

Program design

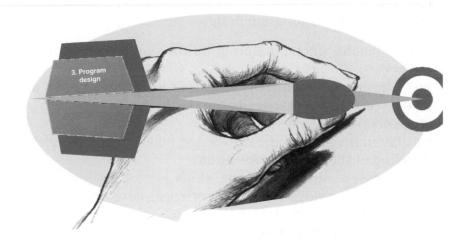

"Oh for a muse of fire that would ascend the brightest heaven of invention!" (*Henry V*: William Shakespeare)

The focus during the design of customized programs is on addressing specified corporate-specific development gaps in a manner that is in keeping with the culture of the commissioning organization. The program has to "fit" into the existing "system" if it is to be truly transformational.

Having established the aim of the program, the "to be" to which the program must contribute, the design process serves to assess, relative to that aim, the organization's "as is". By comparison, the development gap and the customized program's remit is defined.

Clearly there is only one place to start: in the corporate itself. Borrowing from Abraham Lincoln's Gettysburg Address, the design of made-to-measure programs must be seen to be "**of the people, by the people, for the people**". Only thus will it be truly owned by those whom it endeavors to develop. With that comes its validity, necessary for impactful and transformational interventions.

Design therefore begins not only with the corporate but also with the population that the program endeavors to serve and develop. **Two implicated populations** within the organization arise – that of:

- program participants whose own development is the target of the investment
- senior players, and especially immediate managers, for whom program participants are key players in the present and future success of the corporation.

These two populations are the direct beneficiaries of the fit-for-purpose program. Both must commit, own the program, for it to serve the purposes for which it was intended and yield strong returns through application of learning.

Two additional **impacted populations** exist within the organization whose input and insight is invaluable:

- The internal "learning and development" team, a large part of whose role is the development of internal talent for the strategic purposes of the organization.
- The direct reports of intended program participants. As direct recipients of the management/leadership style of program participants, these have first hand experience of being managed by that cadre and are thus uniquely able to identify development needs unseen by more senior players.

Accordingly, canvassing the opinions and needs of the above, particularly of the possible participants and participants' managers, becomes the starting point of design. **Focus groups** and **one-to-one sessions** with representatives from these populations clarify the range of subjects to be covered. Through these sessions we also understand the depth to be explored within individual subjects and the interdependence of emerging topics. With this comes an outside–in view of the organization's internal value chain.

To capture an even larger voice, **questionnaires** that revolve around the preliminary synthesis of focus groups can be sent to a larger percentage of the target and manager populations. These serve to inform the relative importance of the different program subjects. They also serve to capture a population's perceived capability in the areas the program endeavors to develop.

Invariably, through these design activities, we begin to understand what key words mean within the organization and what the desired behaviors look like. As a professional tailor would measure each unique client for his/her selected made-to-measure garment (alias program), so too the program director seeks through the design phase to establish program proportions. To extend the analogy, if the aim can be compared to the human "waist" and the corporate's strategy to the navel: where does the program's true "waist" lie (i.e. above or below the navel)? How "fitted" is the client prepared to actually let you make it? How far below that "waist" should it extend? During the design phase, these nuances must be agreed.

To get a good result, professional tailors do several fittings. So too must the program director or the design team assess the needs of the organization on multiple occasions. One focus group on its own rarely suffices.

The above populations should be seen separately to get honest input. By contrast and in addition, combining populations into one focus group gives valuable insight into the way populations relate to each other. Diversity of opinion – between focus groups, between these and the one-to-ones and from within combined focus groups – makes for a rigorous approach. It also tests meaning and the flexibility of the program specificities to meet the needs of the broader organization. To this end, multiple focus groups from the different populations are essential. By contrast, one-to-ones tend to be fewer, largely confined to the more senior members of the commissioning and the "participants' managers" populations.

The above conveys a scientific approach. Like a research scientist, focus groups serve as organizational Petri dishes. Provoked by a few key questions, the culture of the organization can be observed and answers collated.

Much less precise is the meaning drawn from the synthesis of such sessions. It is relatively easy to summarize the answers to set questions and to define from that the subject elements of the program that will ensue. To pull those factual elements into a **storyline** that adds development value requires a certain art. Each program needs a compelling **red thread**, a logical as well as impactful build-up. Without this, executive development falls short of being inspirational, fails to grow from the organization that "is" to create the organization that is "to be".

Naturally, results from these design sessions need to be brought to life for the delivering faculty. From these they must glean not only the content but also the spirit of the program. Something of the corporate culture, and of the nature of the participants that the program will serve, must be captured within the design.

In the words of one academic faculty who has contributed to four of the corporate clients whose case studies complete the final chapter of this book:

My aims as a faculty member cannot be met unless the course is well designed.

I need to know who the audience is and what their needs are so that I can deliver value for them and expect some challenge and testing of my work in return.

Executives always want material that they can use when they return home, and one cannot provide that without understanding the problems and constraints they face. The course director [as principal program designer] plays a key role in interfacing between me and the customer so she/he must know the material I can provide as well as what the customer wants. I have to be able to trust her/him to do this well so our personal relationship is very important.

Professor Rick Mitchell, Visiting Faculty; August 2009.

Before leaving the subject of program design, agree as part of this the look of the material, the **branding** of the program per se. The importance of coherent templates that reflect the dual parentage of the corporate and the delivery partner cannot be overstated. The impact of logos and the ease-of-use of documentation contribute significantly both to those ever-critical first impressions and to the sense of ownership and relevance.

Also agree the principal processes for measuring business benefits and who will be responsible for their implementation.

Finally, don't hesitate to revisit your design if in doubt. Design serves to deliver the aims of the program, not as an end in itself. It should never be "written in stone". Flexibility of design contributes strongly to the longevity of a program, given the constancy of change within today's organizations.

CHAPTER 4

Team capabilities

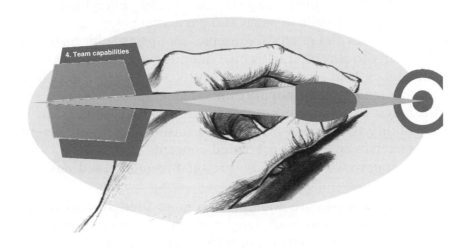

4. Team capabilities

"Horses for courses" (anon)

In the design of a customized intervention, **content** is but one of the crucial elements. Arguably it is a necessary but not sufficient factor to achieve the objectives of an intervention. Yet this is often where the thinking starts. The content **defines** the subject-matter experts, the **faculty**, be they academics, experts or consultants whose practice in the subject area affords them the relevant expertise.

Not that content expertise is the only **criterion** for faculty selection. Each corporate has a style that must, without pretending, be "matched". Most corporates also want faculty who have at least an interest in, if not an in-depth understanding of, the industry in which the corporate operates. Therefore, **subject expertise**, **industry knowledge** and **a "style"** that enables the faculty to work within the culture of the organization form a three-point flexible template for building the team that will deliver program content.

Yet faculty also need a variety of other skills if they are to deliver with impact. These include:

- the ability to engage effectively with participants, inviting them to be partners in the delivery
- the passion for their subjects that brings enjoyment and seduces participants to listen and participate
- the anecdotes and practical examples that bring subjects to life
- the ability to stay on track whilst handling questions that only sometimes lead exactly where faculty want to go, and that more often arrive at inopportune moments
- the magic of being comfortable in one's own authentic skin
- the ability to be open-minded and unshockable as different perspectives emerge on presented concepts
- the energy to work positively through misunderstandings.

Of course these too are additional to more fundamental issues of voice, posture and body language. Faculty need to provide uniquely compelling packages of subject expertise, client curiosity, personal style and delivery excellence.

"Faculty" in its broadest definition includes program directors and the corporate's internal speakers. Let's take each of these in turn.

Not only must the **program director** be able to relate to the client, in order to be the ambassador for the client within the business school and the business school's ambassador within the client, they must also be able to engage credibly with participants during the program. Indeed the role of program director differs quite significantly between different business schools.

For the purposes of this synthesis, the role of the program director is extensive. They:

1. Win the commission.
2. Design the intervention in partnership with the internal-to-the-corporate people development team and the business school faculty.

3. Bring together and inform the faculty cast.
4. Manage and direct the logistics manager.
5. Create the storyline that connects individual contributions during and through the delivery of the program.
6. Ensure that participants follow the "red thread".
7. Manage the overall client relationship with pre, during and post-program client debriefs.

Additionally, program directors add value by:

- facilitating exercises and debriefing key learning at the end of or beginning of each day/module/overall program, and by
- delivering, given their own expertise, content elements of the program.

Finally, as the ever-present business school presence in the program, the program director serves as an:

- executive coach for participants as they, the participants, engage with the individual implications of what the program imparts.

Through this, program directors help participants define the "what", "why" and "how" of ways they will apply the learning, not just in the future but immediately, in the context of their current jobs.

There is one final thing. Program directors also serve the faculty. Quoting from the same regular partner-faculty:

The course director must also ensure that my input interfaces with others', complementing as far as possible and avoiding unplanned overlaps. Academics tend to be rather independent and will always be tempted just to "turn up and do my thing" so the course director has to be assertive about this. I've particularly valued the occasions when all presenters have got together prior to a course to ensure continuity.

Feedback from the course members is important but that of the course director is especially valuable because she/he is in a unique position to a give professional and independent input. I expect her/him to give advice on possible mid-term adjustments as well as with constructive review afterwards.

　　　　Professor Rick Mitchell, Visiting Faculty; August 2009.

Corporate speakers, senior directors/vice presidents or "experts" from the commissioning organization, add great value as **endorsers** of the program. Their presence tells participants that the program is strategic and that the corporate expects them to use the learning to add greater value within their business units. Corporate speakers are often subject experts in their own right, both internally and in the industry at large. Thus their input can be of the same structured relevance as that of business school faculty, so much so that they are often referred to as "corporate faculty".

Corporate speakers can double as **mentors** for participants, especially as they themselves experience something of the development journey by contributing to the program. They become part of the "club" and personally benefit from off-line conversations with participants and faculty alike.

Arguably the most important value that corporate speakers bring is their unique ability to **ground the program content into the corporate's reality**. To this end, exchanges between business school faculty and corporate speakers before the sessions help align messages and validate the detail, and focus and emphasize the content elements.

To be effective, corporate speakers need to be:

- known and highly respected experts within the organization, and/or
- more "senior" than participants, preferably at least two levels higher if in a line structure
- visibly successful (have a track record) in the businesses they manage
- role models of leadership behavior in keeping with the corporate's culture
- well networked within the organization
- engaging in their delivery style, and
- available.

Upholding the structure of great programs are the often-unsung logistics heroes. A vital part of the program "team", these **project or event managers** need to be as **detailed** as they are **creative**, as **operational** as they are **personable**, as **proactive** in anticipating the needs of the program director, faculty and participants as they are **responsive**, particularly on the program days, to changes in arrangements. Participants need clarity regarding arrangements, occasionally support before and during the program. The logistics or event manager serves this purpose. They are also well placed to manage the "production" of program material – gathering materials from faculty, transposing them into program-logoed formats and producing them for participants. **Perseverant** and **precise** in the collation of program materials, they also need to be **creative** as they oversee presentation of the same.

CHAPTER 5

Faculty – subject experts

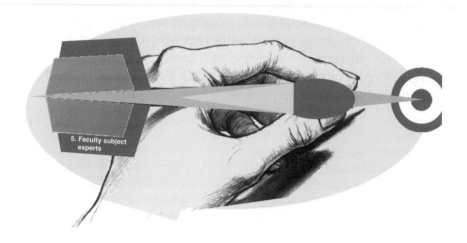

"We come nearest to the great when we are great in humility" (Rabindranath Tagore)

How then do development partners engage faculty, those all-important knowledge and skill merchants?

It comes as no surprise that **what gets measured gets done**, **what gets rewarded gets attention**. Reward can be intrinsic – "the work in itself is energizing" – or extrinsic – "we get paid X per session so it's worth doing."[1]

Faculty, internal or external to the business school, are attracted by both the intrinsic and the extrinsic. Experience however suggests that for subject experts, when the executive development commission is inherently attractive, the tangible reward for engaging with it is significantly less important. You must then question the value of their contribution if money is the primary or only attractor.

Putting to one side the emotive humanity of individual faculty, often their primary interest is purely and simply the relevance of their subject in the context of the commissioning organization. What excites them is the **opportunity to further explore/research their area of expertise** or **to promote it and their understanding within it to those who can further the practice of their ideas**. They want to see their ideas sprout arms and legs. *"Oracle is an extremely forceful organization within the IT industry … I hope I gave [participants] something to think about and a way to approach their next strategic implementation."* (Dr Dina Gray, Visiting Faculty; August 2009)

Faculty, like laboratory scientists, also love to **test their frameworks in environments where that knowledge can yield results**. *"As the creator of SPM,[2] I was very interested in the opportunity to use the model with a population of managers who are currently challenged in their work experience by the growing issue of understanding cultural difference."* (Dr Gilles Spony, Visiting Faculty; August 2009)

It stands to reason that **the corporate itself, its business or the development challenge that the corporate poses**, in relation to the faculty's specialist subject, is the ultimate attractor of the best faculty to executive development programs. *"I have worked with … L'Oréal before and it was an interesting assignment. An issue gets raised that provokes questions that you have never considered before. This can prompt thoughts and explorations that may result in new thinking."* (Professor Cliff Bowman; August 2009)

Certainly, there is no difficulty in securing faculty commitment to executive interventions when their **subject is a prime plank in the corporate's strategy**. *"L'Oréal's CEO Jean-Paul Agon has said that he wants his country managers to be 'ambassadors' for L'Oréal. The company has made sustainable development one of its core business goals. It is crucial, therefore, that the country managers understand what sustainable development means for L'Oréal."[3]* (Professor David Grayson; August 2009)

Faculty like to be **associated with successful programs**. The track record of an executive development team in delivering effective programs and the relationships of trust between those in the executive development team and the individual faculty contribute to the faculty's willingness to engage. *"If you are running the show I know it will be a highly professional program, which I would be happy to be associated with."* (Professor Cliff Bowman; August 2009)

The **actual design, run length and positioning of a program within the corporate** are also faculty attractors. *"It was a pleasure to work with L'Oréal, which I happen to have known for quite a while. Moreover this lecture was taking place in the context of an interesting and integrated process of management development. Thus it was not just a kind of a one-shot thing."* (Professor Maurice Thévenet, ESSEC Business School, Paris; August 2009)

Finally, **programs that promise to deliver measurable business benefits, including close collaboration with internal senior players who are operationally responsible for the practice of the subject being taught**, excite faculty. *"One of the most appealing aspects of this work was the opportunity to work on a program that had the potential for real business impact. I also wanted the opportunity to co-produce the program with Sellafield subject-matter experts. Combining academic theory, models and frameworks with Sellafield-specific inputs, examples and anecdotes has worked well."* (Dr David Denyer; August 2009)

In all of the above cases, a prime faculty challenge is for them to limit their contribution to the allotted time and to deliver that contribution in a give-and-take manner with those participating executives who will themselves have views on what then becomes a shared precious subject.

Faculty quotes embedded into the corporate mini-cases in Chapter 7 elaborate on the above factors. In summary though, attractors are program elements that "reflect well on me/us" and include, in the following categories:

- Client, organization or industry-specific factors:
  - interesting client
  - high-profile assignment
  - potential for high impact and business benefits

- opportunity to closely collaborate with operationally responsible senior players.
- Subject-related items:
  - related to specific faculty's research interest
  - possibility of conducting further research within the client organization or amongst participants
  - sense of being respected for expertise and relevance.
- Program-team considerations:
  - professionally organized event
  - respect for the program director and the executive development team.

It stands to reason that detractors are the absence of the above. Additionally, it is very difficult to secure the contribution of effective faculty where the following apply:

- Contribution to executive development programs is unrecognized within the delivery organization, as is often the case in some business schools where "research-based activity and publication" is the primary source of recognition, promotion and reward.
- Commissioned programs are unproductive as a consequence of unempowered, uninterested and/or disengaged participants.
- Programs are micro-managed in a manner that denies or undermines the faculty and their expertise.
- Fear of failure exists on the part of the faculty. Executive development sessions are more unpredictable than accredited (MBA, MSc) sessions. The fear of real-life questions, never mind those from the devil's advocate, and the all-too-real absence of clear answers is a major deterrent for many.

A key feature of the role of a **program director** is to respond to and manage the above detractors in real-time. It is also their responsibility to **ensure** that the **attractors are hard-wired into the design and delivery of the program**. Through their presence in the live delivery of executive interventions, program directors work with faculty experts to ensure participants' needs are met and mutual respect is engendered whilst the subjects are justly explored in what are always dynamic settings.

To quote one faculty in full on his reason for engagement and his personal take-away from so doing:

Innovation management is a broad and rather diffuse subject.

The problem is always how to deliver content that is useful to the audience, rather than merely interesting. And this difficulty is precisely what makes teaching practitioners so valuable for a faculty member because it constantly pulls one's work back to the real world.

As a presenter, one's relationship with the course director is very important. You want to have confidence that you will be able to do a good job and that requires that the course will be well structured and appropriate to the customer. There is no way a presenter can judge in advance how well it has been done, so you have to be able to trust the course director.

So why does one as a faculty member undertake to teach on a customized executive training course?

1. *Because one enjoys the experience and the challenge of teaching.*
2. *Because it's a good thing to do: teaching is a core part of the role of an academic institution.*
3. *It provides an important test of the validity of one's work. Academic work in management studies is of dubious worth if it is not of value to practitioners. Teaching, along with consultancy, is the laboratory in which one tests one's ideas.*
4. *It may make some money for oneself and/or one's department.*
5. *It often generates useful contacts.*

                   Professor Rick Mitchell, visiting faculty; August 2009

CHAPTER 6

Program components

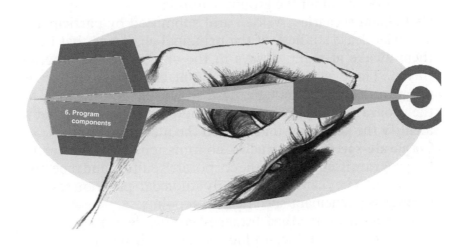

"Float like a butterfly, sting like a bee" (Muhammad Ali)

Having said that **content** is a necessary but not sufficient element of program success, what else should one consider? Most people, and particularly adults, learn best when they personally engage, when they are implicated. That is what makes "**experience**" such a powerful teacher. The more "**action**" there is in the "**learning**", the greater the relevance and retention. Though this is by no means a comprehensive list, the additional **program components**, some of which are elaborated through the client synopses of Chapter 9, contribute greatly:

- **Pre-program questionnaires** (e.g. "learning contracts") position the participants' expertise and preferences relative to the program and before arrival. When synthesized these serve to prepare participants for the experience they will undertake.

More importantly, and of immense value, results from these offer faculty, and program directors in particular, a unique insight to the challenges, hopes and expectations of individual participants and of the group as a whole.

- **"Webinars"** in advance of the program prepare participants and engage their managers. By outlining the program in advance and tabling questions, they ensure that the start on the first face-to-face day is already dynamic, the proverbial ice is broken, all hit the ground running.

- **Participant scenarios**, written and submitted by participants, are brief "case studies" of the principal challenge that keeps them awake at night, always in the context of the program theme. These serve as the first point of application for the program learning. Though these should be confidential, for the program director's eyes only, they can be summarized to identify the key issues that burden the incoming group.

- **Corporate-specific case studies**, commissioned and written for the program itself, capture the corporate's culture and repeating situations. They can be collectively studied in program sessions to discuss participant-specific action points.

- **E-learning, networked and distance-learning elements** (webinars, podcasts) support face-to-face sessions, bring participants to a shared understanding of program subjects and facilitate faster learning.

- **Pre-reading**, including **articles and case studies**, brings all participants to a "level playing field" before the program starts and focuses them on the subjects that will be treated.

- **Psychometrics and 360°s** diagnose individuals' preferences and perspectives, enabling conversations to be specific and program input to be personalized by the participants themselves and, if relevant, coaches.

- **Assessment and development centers** allow corporates to categorize their talent in terms of development needs and to design or identify appropriate interventions that support individual development pathways in the context of succession plans.

- **Coaching**, before, during and after the program, provides for structured, evidence-based, objective conversations. Often these sessions raise new levels of awareness. At their best, they enable participants to identify for themselves their options and to decide for themselves their actions.

- **Small group/syndicate work**, preferably built into each half-day of the program, creates the space for individuals to apply the learning to their corporate. Through these sessions, participants make sense, in a team context, of the taught elements and the plenary discussions. These are essential for participants to own the "learning" and to commit to action.
- **Triad or paired work** enables participants to work through more personal content sessions. Action is the end-goal. These sessions allow for greater honesty when answering the "so what" that often follows a thought-provoking session.
- **Video-work** provides evidence for structured feedback. Working with a coach or with a peer (in pairs or triads), the benefit of seeing yourself as filmed, on film, whether it is in a one-to-one exchange with a neutral third party or in a groupwork session, is electric. Your own chance to see yourself as you actually come across, to be the proverbial "fly on the wall", provides an undeniably rich opportunity for personal awareness.
- **Learning logs** encourage participants to document key thoughts at the end of each day and to summarize at the end of the program the key learnings, how these might be applied in their day-job, and what they've learnt about themselves/others/their corporate during the sessions. These are "for the individual participant's eyes only". Program directors have "visitation rights" but only if allowed by the participant.
- **Business simulations** provide an action-learning experience, be it focused on strategy or a specific discipline such as project management, which enables participants to gain a helicopter yet hands-on perspective on classic and generic whole-of-business situations.
- **Real projects**, either selected by the participants or credibly identified by the senior team, enable you to create action-learning environments. Such projects become the first-point of application of learning and the focus for in-session and often inter-modular groupwork.
- **Actors or storytellers** enacting a myth or storyline guide participants to develop the skills of bringing events to life. They also provide a structure for unpacking one's leadership journey – past, present and projected – in a manner that engages participants holistically: mind, body and soul.

- **Creative sessions** where participants write a poem, paint, sculpt or construct a piece of music can be powerful vehicles for expression that tap into new depths of passion.
- **Evening and daytime out-of-the-box activity** open participants to think creatively. They also lubricate the formation of learning networks from what is often a motley group.
- **Modules** per se allow business schools to see participants (and for them to see each other) more than once over an extended period of time, to challenge their progress and commitment to the learning. They create a built-in accountability structure, providing a number of opportunities for goal-setting and assessment of the application of the learning.
- **Program pictures and storylines** introduced at the beginning of the program serve as a "litmus test" for ensuring participants' understanding and for drawing interim summaries.
- **Evaluation forms and mechanisms for tracking return on investment** are essential. Integrity demands no less, from both the business school and the participants. Measuring the impact of a program is easier to the extent that it is tool-based, but even highly subjective leadership-focused interventions should be expected to deliver quantifiable differences to the funding corporate. The key question remains: "What specifically did you learn on the program that you have applied in your day job, and to what benefit?"
- **Post-program follow-up sessions**, from "alumni events" to simple one-to-ones, can serve to keep the learning and the networks alive, to provoke application of learning as some share what they have put into practice, and to update thinking on rapidly evolving subjects.

No one program contains all of the above, not least because all of the above would not be palatable to most corporates. The skill of the program director is to blend the right elements in the appropriate proportions, guided principally by the objectives of the intervention, the strategy of the organization, the culture of the corporate, the nature of the participants and the time allowed for the intervention.

Within the program syntheses of our six corporates you will find briefly listed the main design components that make up the DNA of each.

Thus at the heart and at the start of all customized interventions there are a series of design exercises to define the principal program components in light of the all-important:

- AIM and STRATEGIC CONTEXT of the corporate
- BOUNDARIES of the remit
- BUDGET that will underpin the intervention
- Corporate RESOURCES that will support it
- CULTURE that will embrace it
- TIME FRAME in which it has to operate and deliver, and
- ASPIRATIONS and ABILITIES of those who will attend.

Clearly the CAPABILITY of the business school to deliver is only a limiting factor if the faculty comes exclusively from those employed full-time by the business school itself. This is increasingly rare. The only limiting factor for most credible business schools is the program director's or business school's network of subject experts and the corporate's budget, given the variable day-rate of external "faculty".

Having said all of the above, it is as important to state what a program *will not do or deliver* as it is to specify *what it will contain*. Many poor relationships ensue where this has not been clarified from the start.

CHAPTER 7

Stages to program delivery

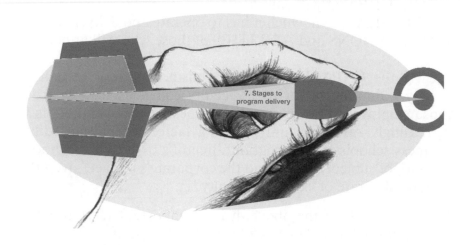

"A stitch in time saves nine" (anon)

What then are the consecutive steps for those whose task it is to win, design, direct and deliver customized programs? Though central at every point is the service of clients, and within that the development of purposeful relationships remains the prime responsibility, key skills differ from one phase to another.

If this were to serve as a personal note titled **"the seven-steps to customized executive development"**, it might read as follows:

A. In order to stand a good chance of winning the commission, it isn't enough to deliver to the letter of the request. Nor is it sufficient to connect at a personal level with the selection panel or decision-maker. The element of surprise, the ability to propose something different that captures the imagination of the commissioning team, *whilst concurrently* giving confidence that the aims for which the program is intended will be delivered, can be compelling.

Begin therefore as the external party and expert in executive development that you are, recognizing that the greatest value initially comes from casting fresh eyes on the commissioning organization. Contextualize that to the "request for proposal" (RFP) and emerging response. Let experience underpin boldly innovative ideas, always ensuring they are appropriate to the remit being explored.

At the same time, particularly when stretching the boundaries of your offering, use everything at your disposal to understand the culture of the prospective-client organization. Match your embryonic ideas to that. As one brilliant faculty put it: "If you have unconventional ideas, wear conventional clothing."[1]

Read the RFP[2] without pre-conception. Resist the temptation to superimpose a prior program design on what first presents as the requirement.

Although RFPs differ greatly in clarity, what is actually written should be taken as the basics for the desired intervention. Beyond that, consider what lies "between the lines" of the official document. Whenever possible, speak to the corporate spokesperson or the commissioning team to gain that insight. Amongst the key questions to ask is: "Why are you considering investing in this development at this point in time?"

Ideas quickly begin to form, particularly for those experienced in the design of executive development. Again, hold back.

In a logically packaged manner, detail what from your perspective is being requested. Concurrently, create a big-picture concept that states clearly: "This program must enable participants to ..." Together these two elements constitute the backbone of an initial draft design. Whenever possible, reflect this back to the commissioning client before embellishment.

With that in mind, consider more fully the corporate's strategic context. Identify the industry in which the corporate operates, the major challenges it faces therein, its opportunities and constraints, its principal competitors. Summarize the corporate's history in that ecosystem. Consider how this corporate's intervention could/should impact on such a scenario.

Map and whenever possible connect with significant stakeholders. Pinpoint what they need and want from the intervention in question. Build that into the offering, not as additions but as integrated elements of the intervention.

Reconcile the RFP and your emerging response to the strategic context. Consider, if suggested by the strategic context, any additional elements to the proposed intervention. Alternatively, use this strategic understanding to reposition your proposed response, to better angle its value-adding potential for the commissioning client.

Even if this can only happen as the opening gambit of the formal presentation, check your understanding of the depth and breadth of the requirement as early in the process as possible. This is the first step in building a working rapport with the commissioning team. Successful interventions are built on trust. Trust starts with honest exchanges between the commissioning team, who understand the organization from the inside, and the delivery organization, whose external expertise is sought.

B. **In designing the intervention**, several disciplines come into play.

Firstly, consider what specific terms and content-subjects "look like" in the commissioning organization. Take a term like *"partnering"*, which frequently appears in corporates' executive development demands. To "partner" effectively in a highly competitive, matrixed internal environment requires, amongst other things, clear *performance measurement*. These work to ensure successes are appropriately attributed to multiple parties[3] within often competing business units without double-counting at the corporate level. By contrast, to "partner" in a consortium-working environment,[4] separate entities must collaborate in a *"projectized"* manner to deliver a seamless whole. Such a systemic approach is necessary to ensure that the delivery from each individual party dovetails appropriately with that of all relevant others. Though both aspects of "partnership" are important, each requires a different discipline with its unique tools and frameworks.

Secondly, to better understand what is required, it helps to identify "exemplars", from within or from outside of the organization, individuals who embody these terms, who display the skills the program is intended to develop.

As early as possible, timetable the emerging design. Time is the most measurable of factors. Most commissioning entities will have an idea of the length of the program they are considering. It may simply boil down to: "For how long are you willing to release your executives?" Given that most topics within executive development programs can individually be studied to PhD level, program design is strongly influenced by the length of time you have for interconnected exploration of what are almost always substantial concepts.

Added to the perennial pressure on time, behavioral change is what corporates almost always actually require. Even with the most cerebral of programs, success lies in the extent to which participants behave differently – be it in how they think, how they take action or how they relate to others – as a consequence of attending the program. Thus, if behavioral change is to be achieved, the program has to do more than impart knowledge. It must also convince participants that they personally need to change, to engage with that knowledge in a new way. What participants "experience" during the program influences their "take-away" and contributes strongly to this personal "commitment to development". It goes beyond "education" (however undoubtedly worthwhile that is as a stand-alone). Agree the program "experience" elements with the corporate project team and allocate appropriate time for the same.

At key junctions, continue to validate with the commissioning team the refining big-picture concept. Work whenever possible with the prime sponsor as you iterate through to the detail of the "blueprint design".

Once the blueprint design is agreed, refine and confirm detailed content through focus groups and one-to-one sessions. Include key stakeholders and the sponsor. Though the program is intended to usher in a "new thing" and the internal-to-the-corporate commissioning team should know best, ensure that what you are proposing is "palatable", is capable of "fitting" those for whom it is intended. To this end, focus groups should include representatives of the target population as well as representatives of the target population's direct reports and of their managers.

Having done this, begin to align the confirmed design, the big picture and the refined detail, to potential faculty. Ensure that these are not only subject-matter experts but wherever possible individuals who have an interest in the corporate and experience of the corporate's industry. Delivery style is also important.

Because faculty are never compelled to deliver, think about how to best hook them. Consider what might be the angle by which the proposed program most contributes to the faculty's own interests. Debrief preferred faculty with this in mind, knowing that they will have to make their sessions their own, in accordance with their convictions, passion and subject-matter expertise. As part of this, they will need the freedom to explore their subject with the corporate, albeit within the boundaries of the now confirmed design.

Ultimately, each faculty's material should contain: an answer to the "so what" question, stating that "By the end of this session, participants will ..."; key tools; detailed breakout sessions; key corporate-contextualizing examples, exercises or mini case studies; linkages to connected sessions within the program; recommendations for further reading. An item of pre-reading or preparatory work is welcome but optional.

To provide the best chance of measuring business benefits, the process for following-up application of learning should be built into the program. Templates to this end should be drafted as part of the program design. As part of this, agree what follow-up activity will be the responsibility of the corporate's development team and which will be owned by the external development partner.

C. **In order to integrate faculty**, engage them as early as possible in the emerging design. To the extent that individual faculty stand out from the beginning as possible contributors, and at the risk of not being able to include them in the final delivery team if the design changes, seek their input and feedback on the design as it emerges through the above process.

Some development experts include faculty from receipt of the RFP and in the initial pitch to win the commission. Occasionally clients specifically ask for faculty inclusion in the bidding presentation, to get a feel for the caliber of the proposed delivery team. This does risk short-circuiting the design process as it presents the commissioning team with an almost "fait accompli". The danger is that you not only propose at the final client presentation the overall design concept and content, but that you also fix the nuance of the subject and the style of the program by selecting the principal faculty deliverers.

Yet faculty must be engaged wholeheartedly, and the sooner you involve them the more certain you are of achieving that. They must feel like the central program partners that they are, free and valued as vital expert contributors.

To this end, and at the very latest once the design has been confirmed and the preferred faculty has agreed to contribute, meetings must be arranged (by phone or face to face) between faculty and the commissioning team. Faculty also need to be connected with the corporate's internal subject-matter experts. Through these exchanges, faculty refine their input and identify the relevant aspects of their portfolio that will feature in the specific program. Whenever appropriate, faculty may develop new material (case studies, diagnostic tools) specifically for the intervention. The power of this cannot be overstated.

Faculty stand as individuals. Participants, however, experience them individually and as a team. Exactly because each brings unique input, faculty need to make their messages connect with the overall program storyline. Pre-program faculty team meetings, hard though they are to arrange, therefore serve to align messages. Through these, the faculty team develops a systemic perspective across the intervention as a whole. Faculty can then individually signpost to and reference each other's key messages, building on each others' session progressively. The richness that this imparts to participants is often tangible.

Additional to the meeting of all faculty, or faculty sub-meetings on related subjects, a set of the top five slides that summarize each session should be held as a shared program resource. Passed between faculty, these collectively reinforce the overall program message. As a post-program "gift", they also serve as a program summary for participants.

D. In preparing for delivery, consider and be sure to manage as program director the following:

- Room layout – Pay regard to participants' personal space.
- Breakout rooms – These should be close enough to the main room to enable faculty to speedily facilitate all groups.
- Participants' material – This will include a slide-pack and learning log as well as paper, pens, memory stick, "wallet" – and must be purposeful and complete.
- Delivery aids – These may include a projector, computer, OHP, flip charts, posters, white boards, Post-its, Blu-Tack, water.
- Room temperature – This should be regulated to suit different tastes; a bit on the cool side keeps all alert.
- Comfort breaks – These should be part of the morning coffee and afternoon tea routine, though participants are always free to avail themselves as necessary.
- Lunch arrangements – Between 12:30 and 13:00 is ideal. You want the development challenge to come from the new thinking, not from human fundamental needs that distract. Cater for food allergies and be aware of religious considerations such as Ramadan.
- Evening and teaming activities – These add enormously to the "feel-good" factor but more importantly make for great networking opportunities. To focus discussions around the program, consider introducing a strategic question on which you'll take feedback at the start of the next day.
- Warm-up "exercises" – Brainteasers or fun group exercises that allow you to observe individuals' behavior relative to the program's aim serve multiple purposes. They also break the awkwardness of first encounters.

E. Once actual delivery commences, be aware of and regulate atmospheric issues, specifically the room temperature and lighting.

Trickier is the business of directing delivery pace and volume. Agree with each faculty your signaling mechanism but use it only as a last resort. Even unseen by participants (if you are operating from the back of the room), signaling can seriously affect a faculty's performance. Not only does it distract them but it also pressurizes them to try to change what are often intuitive aspects of personal delivery.

Notwithstanding, having agreed the need to involve participants from the start, and having designed into the program the faculty-initiated and session-specific ways of so doing, keep a watch on participant involvement. Silence on their part is not an issue if their body language speaks of engagement. If otherwise, beware. Work within what you have agreed with the faculty but look to provoke a reaction, elicit commentary or start discussion between participants and the faculty. Value from the session is as dependent on what participants contribute as it is on the input from faculty. Learning works best in a participative social context.

To this end, honor the time set aside for breakout sessions. It is not easy for faculty to stick to their allotted times, especially if participant discussion is lively. Faculty bring a wealth of subject information and a passion for that subject which makes it difficult for them not to add to their delivery even whilst in the process of delivering that in person. These factors need to be considered when designing the session and whilst opportunities should be seized, that design must also be respected. If not, breakout sessions are likely to be sacrificed, even though these offer the first chance for discussing and clarifying how the learning of that session can be applied in the workplace. This should not be lightly abandoned. Participant buy-in may also be compromised. Without breakout sessions, participants often disengage and feel "talked at". Exceptions to this are rare, and found almost exclusively among renowned gurus whose infotainment (exceptional ground-breaking content and/or entertaining presentation styles) holds attention. Even then, transfer of learning to the workplace is threatened, given that it is rarely facilitated except through activities such as breakouts and ensuing faculty debriefs.

F. In the pursuit of business benefits, conclude each module or program with a summary of the key learning. Not only does this demand a clear synthesis from the program director about what has been imparted/taught, it also requires an identification of key learnings by participants. To this end, build in time for reflection, for completion of individual learning logs. Follow this with small-group work so that participants can share and discuss possible application. This process brings to the surface the topics/learning that several have identified as important. Concurrently, it creates a sense of accountability to put the learning into practice. This learning-capture process should be driven by the program director as the principal red-thread activity.

To support application and continuity of learning, recap with the corporate commissioning team what you as the external delivery partner will do by way of post-delivery follow-up. The mechanisms and generic formats for this should have formed part of the program's design. Refine those in the light of discussions that emerge during actual program delivery.

Inform participants as early in the delivery process as possible of what is planned by way of follow-up. That way it comes as no surprise. This in itself serves to condition participants' approach to the program from the start and reinforces application of learning. Having said that, experience suggests that people don't do what you expect; they do what you inspect.

Schedule agreed activity, according to assigned responsibilities (the delivery partners v. the corporate's internal development team), through phone calls, emails or face-to-face sessions. Hopefully, activity will not consist of a single contact though it has to be time-bound and proportionate to the program itself. A rule of thumb is to organize the first post-program contact no more than three months following program completion. This provides sufficient time for participants to have trialled something, insufficient time for cynicism to set in if they haven't.

A second and maybe third assessment-of-learning session can then follow six and 12 months after program completion. Each follow-up session should be different to spur creativity and maximize participant engagement. Each should nevertheless capture application and benefits gained.

As inferred above, additional to what you as a development partner do by way of follow-up, there are a collection of activities that the commissioning team can and should deliver. Examples of these include brown-bag lunches with a director, business projects that can be worked through during parallel application workshops, best practice clubs to discuss application of learning in the context of key organizational development themes, and individual synthesis reports to track tools applied and resulting benefits.

Confirm with the client organization the processes that they will own and pursue as internal follow-up activity. Confirm that which you as delivery partner will provide. Work collaboratively with your commissioning partners to ensure that all follow-up activity is appropriate and joined-up, that benefits are not only collated but also validated by credible senior third parties within the organization.

Notwithstanding the above, remember to debrief the commissioning client and program sponsor at key junctions and soon after program completion. A clearly specified approach to follow-up is no substitute for timely conversations that underpin trust and allay fears. Use this debrief as an opportunity to be the first to share issues and difficulties that arose during the delivery, especially when those issues and difficulties are of your own making, as the delivery partner. Our humanity is forgivable as long as we own up and address the causes proactively. Where the issues are of the participants' making, be careful to honor the confidentiality of individual participants. Position the challenge as one that needs to be managed in the spirit of partnership between the delivery partner and the commissioning corporate. Use it as an opportunity to better address the needs of the target population. Agree necessary design changes and action.

G. And so, on that note, it's full circle return to the oxymoron of what some call **client management** – as if a client could actually be managed. I prefer to think of it as the call to continuously engage with the client with the purpose and in the hope of adding increasingly rare value – for the corporate and the delivery partners.

At its heart, this is a process of ongoing dialogue, both of the planned and of the spontaneous variety. Through this comes the weaving of unique shared histories, deeper understanding of the client's internal issues, sharpened delivery, broadened relationships, leveraged benefits.

As for content of the ongoing dialogue, these are busy professionals.

- Look for ways to legitimately inform your key contacts' thinking.
- Whenever possible, and without charging, channel market-specific insight to key players and participants as relevant and appropriate.
- Deliver on promises without delay.
- Contribute to reflections when asked for input to new situations, especially when those impact on the content or processes of live programs.
- Invite key corporate players (corporate speakers or ex-program participants) to contribute to your organizational activities. Their involvement in your endeavors endorses you as a delivery partner; it creates a living reference for other clients as well as for the client-specific program within the organization.

All of the above must emerge from a genuine passion for the client and their challenges. Without that, manipulation will rightly be suspected and resented.

Corporate clients are giants. Their executives targeted for development are on the whole brilliant, highly educated, resourceful, confident, fully occupied, no-nonsense, experienced individuals. Working with them is a privilege, the invitation to engage with them an honor.

CHAPTER 8

Measuring business benefits

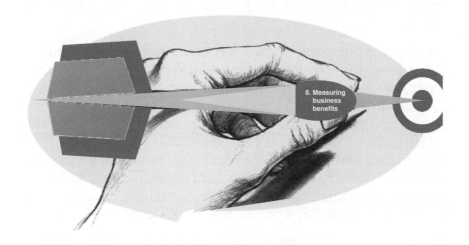

"Faced with what is right, to leave it undone shows
lack of courage" (Confucius)

As noted in comments peppered through the previous chapters,
every educational or development activity should specify from
the start the new skills or behaviors that participants are expected
to display as a consequence of interventions. Without clarity on
this, development activity is spurious and its results are at the
very best unquantifiable.

The key questions in this regard are:

1. What, as a consequence of the program, does the client
   organization want:
   • participants to be able to do or no longer to do?
   • the organization to deliver or eliminate?
   • that is new to the organization as it currently exists?

2. Over what time frame?
3. With what milestones?

Put simply, one client organization's director is known to regularly ask participants who completed development programs: "What are you doing differently?"

The more precise the answers to these questions, the clearer the commissioning client is about the outcome that is wanted from a program, the more certain the client organization is to obtain a payback.

The expected outcome from a program goes well beyond the end-of-program evaluation that simply assesses the initial impact of the session. Best practice demands that delivery is assessed through end-of-session feedback sheets that give a feel for the immediate impact of the experience; but measurable benefit goes beyond this. It consists of that which results from participants' application of the learning. Only through this can **quantifiable value** be added to the client organization. This added value must be incremental, value that would not have occurred had the development intervention not taken place.

Yet, without a "**control group**", as often used in scientific experiments, that in itself is going through the same challenges and transformation as the group undertaking the development program, the specific effect of a development program on the success of the organization undertaking the intervention is not an easy thing to isolate or measure.

Working a generic example, if the ultimate aim of a program is to enhance "economic performance", the new skills are those that result in an increase of sales and/or decrease in operating costs and/or tightening of working capital and/or lowering of external charges, including taxes, and/or reduction in the capital intensity of operations. Though there is always a time lag between applying the learning and seeing a result, and that result may initially be negative as certain concepts that are trialed inevitably fail, tracking such improvements within the remits of program participants is relatively easy to do.

Even so, improvement in results is seldom the effect of just one action or change of approach. At best one can only truthfully say that an executive program was one of several contributors to an improvement in performance *in the period immediately following* specific interventions. Clearly the above applies to an even greater extent when it comes to programs whose purpose is to enhance a population's "strategic thinking" or their "leadership skills".

Take another example from the other end of the spectrum – "leadership skills" programs. The brief for most leadership development interventions is to grow the future leaders of the commissioning organization. Sometimes a time-scale is set, with "three to five years from now" being common. Program content is structured to enhance the existing strengths, maybe also to develop in participants desired leadership aspects that are currently less evident. (Desired leadership aspects may not be missing; they may simply not be surfacing.)

However well the program is designed, however well the development partner delivers, however impactful the intervention, enhanced leadership skills alone do not make for internal promotion. Despite the best succession plans, intangible factors such as social networks, chance encounters and emerging situations conspire to inform the promotion of many.

Leadership briefs can also include the desire to *fidéliser* the troops, to reduce attrition of talent from participant populations. The same logic explored above applies here and works against the efficacy of such programs to guarantee such results. External opportunities unknown at the time of the program may entice star performers to leave the corporate stable.

Thus, whilst over the passage of time one can assess whether or not participants from a given program do actually become the future leaders of the organization, many other variables also play a part. Success or failure of a leadership development program to deliver future leaders is very largely dependent on the larger system within which the program itself unfolds.

Arguably the only bona-fide way of measuring specific quantifiable benefits from an executive development program is to **track benefits from the application of unique tools, models or frameworks taught in the program**. Business benefits from such an approach are evidenced within Sellafield's programs. Though further examples are included in their corporate scenario within Chapter 9, the following serve to demonstrate how tracking the application of specific tools learnt on a program can lead to the identification of specific business benefits.

One of the key themes within Sellafield's customized programs is change management. Using the Cassandra model as a mapping tool,[1] one participant evaluated the benefits that would ensue from a particular new project. They concluded that the project was incapable of delivering the promised benefits. Presented as such, the project was scrapped before it started. This saved £4m, together with six months of a highly skilled expert team that was then freed to address a different critical assignment.

Processes for measuring program benefits include:

- Post-program follow-up sessions that are:
  - run by the development delivery organization
  - run by the client organization's executive development team.
- End-of-program reviews within modular programs that measure the application of learning from earlier modules.
- Post-program application reports (such as the "Far-Sight" report managed by the internal learning and development team at Oracle, one of the six corporates whose programs are synthesized in Chapter 9) request a brief description of applied learning. Related business benefits can be collated as the program's return on investment.
- Alumni events where presentations by exemplars of what they've applied can encourage all to do more.

Fundamentally, the expectation that application of program learning will be tracked and measured to quantify a program's return on investment should be written into the program timetable. Participants, aware from the start that this is a vital feature of the program, will thus look for ways to apply the learning to their reality as the program unfolds. Equally, faculty will be conscious of the need to be practical in their delivery, and relevant to the level of the participants, to ensure that their sessions feature amongst those whose value is tangible to the organization.

Processes and mechanisms for capturing business benefits should be shared by both the development partner and the client organization. Whilst the development partner has the capability and legitimacy to chase application of learning, the client organization has the internal networks and clout to gather participants for such evaluation. Together, working in tandem without duplication, the delivery partner and the corporate are a formidable force in this endeavor.

CHAPTER 9

Case studies: corporate journeys

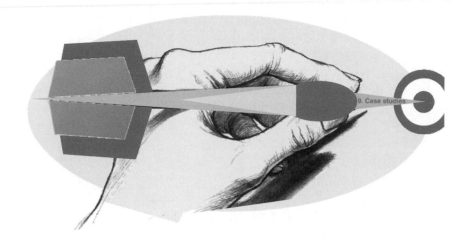

"Our greatest foes [at an individual level], and whom we must chiefly combat, are within" (Miguel de Cervantes)

"To attend to what is simple when one has the mettle to attempt what is difficult is to strip talent of its dignity" (José Marti)

Studies of the customized programs of our six corporates serve to flesh out the preceding chapters. Indeed, the chapters serve to frame the following uniquely significant interventions.

9.1 SMG – Stewart Milne Group

A major regional player

Program ran from December 2003 to May 2005.

Guiding our thoughts stood the program's strap-line: *Equipping all man-managers and leaders to reach their potential – to **be more strategic, better people managers and greater delivers of competitive quality***. For internal promotion it was simplified to "Reaching your potential". Within SMG Group, this program had to raise individuals' capability to fulfill their current roles to the full, to retain the Group's best talent, to unleash their ability to deliver more and more effectively with the resources and people they already had.

The business

The UK pioneer of timber-framed construction systems, Stewart Milne Group was during the duration of the program a privately-owned house-building and construction business. It was also the largest house builder in Scotland. The Group employed 1000 staff and had experienced exponential growth since its inception in 1975. On average they had doubled revenues each five years. Shortly before engaging Cranfield, the Group had expanded to England with the purchase of a timber production facility in Oxford. The limited available pool of suitable talent and the existing operational structure were posing difficult problems.

Facts and figures

In December 2003 the Group's board and divisional directors undertook a Cranfield-facilitated strategy workshop to define the Group's six-year strategic business plan. Following this strategic plan and in order to enable their people to deliver ambitious targets, a customized development program was designed and agreed. Between February 2004 and March 2005, over 240 individuals, a quarter of those employed, attended an integrated series of highly interactive half-day modules delivered in four to seven-day blocks at Cranfield. These centered around three themes: strategic thinking, people management and quality delivery. Each program-block was introduced by the Group's Chairman and concluded by the Managing Director.

The business issues

During the strategy workshop the Group's vision cohered: to become a leading independent UK national designer and provider of homes, recognized for premium-quality customer satisfaction and financial returns. To this end the Group sought to expand construction into England and more than double in size by 2010. Availability of both skilled labor and land with planning consent were recognized as *the* two limiting factors in the pursuit of sustainable growth. The board perceived an opportunity to address the skills shortage by enhancing the ability of the existing management team. Stewart Milne, Chairman and Chief Executive, explained: *"We are committed to providing an environment where our people are given the opportunity to use their technical skills and develop management expertise to attain our goals, in a culture that centers around growth through cohesive teamwork and continuous people development."*

The challenge

In line with the Group's strategic business plan it was vital to equip managers with the capability to undertake larger and more diverse roles. In particular, the development task was to:

- enable all managers to operate more strategically
- enhance managers' effectiveness as leaders of people
- equip managers to deliver quality in an increasingly competitive environment.

The approach

Cranfield, working in close partnership with the Stewart Milne Group HR Manager:

- Directed and facilitated a strategy development workshop with the Group board and divisional boards which resulted in a six-year corporate plan, now updated annually. With this came clarity and "shared meaning" about the desired outcomes from the development intervention.
- Analyzed the Group's 36 management competencies to consolidate these to six critical ones representing three themes. These were reflected in the above-stated objectives of the development program.
- Conducted a series of diagnostic exercises with the top team and a representative selection of managers to validate the development needs.
- Engaged with subject specialists to design and deliver the series of 14 modules that composed the core development program.
- Created and delivered one-day awareness sessions for all employees that had not participated in "the Cranfield experience".

The program

Modules containing tools and frameworks on strategy, people management and quality were delivered in a manner appropriate to the Group's five levels of management: Group board, divisional directors, senior managers, line managers and supervisors.

Tailor-made exercises enabled participants to experience the extent to which they could put new knowledge into practice. Through diverse role-plays and outdoor exercises, individuals became more aware of their natural tendencies to negotiate, plan and implement as well as their inclination to engage with others. Through these sessions, participants explored how they could enhance their effectiveness in their current roles.

The program picture on page 52 summarizes the architecture of this hierarchically cascading program.

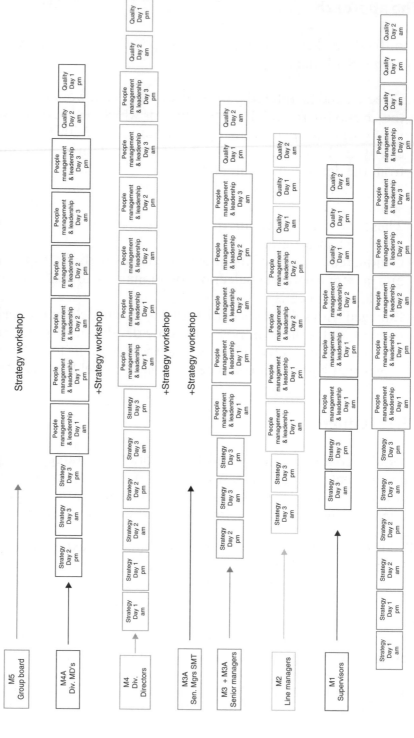

Program picture: a development hierarchy

By way of key to this and to provide a flavor of the content elements the program covered:

Strategy

Day 1 The strategic management process: vision to implementation, corporate v. functional v. BU plans and strategies; stakeholder analysis and brand image.
Day 2 The environment: PEST and Porter's five forces.
Day 3 Strategic assets, SWOTS, culture web; competitive advantage.

People management

Day 1 Authenticity, role of manager, role of leader; delegation, performance management, KPIs, appraisals.
Day 2 Communication, meetings and information management.
Day 3 Conflict resolution, the disciplinary(s), owning up to disappointments; role preferences, group dynamics and personal style.

Quality

Day 1 Customer centricity, drivers of value, continuous improvement culture; process ownership in cross-functional teams.
Day 2 Procedures, processes and milestones.

Thus, in the context of strategy, we took participants on a journey of corporate discovery that started with an external perspective of their market, moved into an analysis of their positioning within that and concluded with heightened awareness of their individual impact on competitiveness.

From that we explored management and leadership. On the agreed understanding that authenticity is essential for sustainable, impactful and credible behavior, we started with them as individual managers and leaders. We considered how their individuality influenced their approach to delegation and accountability, to communication and to the management of different opinions. This led to team and group implications, given the personal styles not only of the participants but also of those they manage, of their own managers and more broadly of those with whom they interacted.

On the home stretch we unpacked the issues surrounding quality, taking this discussion and the application of tools to hierarchical relevance. Beyond the obvious utility of the SMG "product" – the house that must stand and protect its inhabitants from the vagaries and inclemencies of nature – value, like beauty, is in the eyes of the beholder. Participants (from directors to team-leaders) worked with taught frameworks and models to make explicit how they individually drove value relevant to the house buyer and owner.

Everyone did not always engage positively with all sessions at first. One poignant comment made "on the quiet" during a coffee break captured the sentiments of many in the team-leader population on the subject of "strategy": "My job is to nail timber-frame sections together. I take a nail, pick up my hammer, pound it as hard and as many times as necessary to drive that nail into the timber. Once done, I take another nail and start the process all over again. What have I got to do with 'customer value' drivers?" That very question became the starting point of the post-coffee session.

Far from academic, this suite of programs forced participants, faculty and program directors to discover the pragmatic relevance of each session to the level of the hierarchy and the individual with which/whom we engaged.

Making a difference

Some examples of changes brought forward by the program, gathered six months after the program's conclusion:

"As a result of increased discussion, reflection and the application of new tools, an opportunity was identified, within six months of

the start of the program, to save some £1.2 million through better inter-divisional collaboration."

"Discussions have become more structured, with higher expectations of measurability of both intention and action."

"Attitudinal shifts have begun to foster an even stronger 'can do' mentality reflected in a strengthening of business performance."

Writing shortly after the program ended, Karen Catto, then HR Group Manager, said: *"It is vital if we are to achieve our growth plans that we are able to not only attract quality people but retain and maximize the strength of expertise that already exists throughout the group.*

Working in partnership with Cranfield we have in-depth access to world-class specialists on every management subject, as well as in executive development. Involving our managers in the design phase has resulted in a flexible, bespoke program that lays the foundation to meet future challenges."

Return on investment

The first direct result from the program was the development of the Group's first documented, highly participative and analytically derived business plan. As a consequence of implementing this plan, enabled by the ensuing development program depicted above, the Group was able to double its business in three years where previously it had done so every five. Additionally, within a year of the program's completion, the Group consolidated its move into the UK from Scotland, spearheaded by improving results from its Oxfordshire timber-frame factory.

Program components

1. Content – business school faculty.
2. SMG board member's contextualization and contribution.
3. Groupwork to pragmatically apply the learning.
4. Psychometrics to diagnose personal preferences and position diversity.

5. Learning logs to encourage personal reflection and drive application of learning.
6. 360° to Group board members and individual feedback on personal reports.
7. Experiential exercises to encourage out-of-the-box thinking and to bring to the surface habitual behavior.
8. Follow-up debriefs with program sponsors.
9. Follow-up review of benefits gained from the program.

Key corporate sponsors

Stewart Milne, primary shareholder, CEO and Chairman; Karen Catto, Group HR Manager.

Faculty experience

I always liked the idea of working in a complete business, with all its myriad complexity that also imbues the genesis of new business ideas, hopes, fears and combined aspirations expressed through self-selected volunteers who represent a diagonal slice from the business.

The Stewart Milne organization consistently reflects the Cranfield values about the notion of bringing ideas into action that will make a positive difference to business performance and outcomes.

My first engagement with the group seemed to be characterized by a spirited challenge to each other's work culture and approach to getting things done. As the engagement development continued, it was realized that there were many more similarities than differences in our respective modi operandi.

The experience of the sessions was the most memorable aspect of the whole course. Typical highlights of this included the group maintaining the high ground of a psychological contract between members, geared toward learning outcomes. Despite considerable pressures the whole group remained larger than the sum of its parts.

What were the personal gains from the course? For me, a vindication of a few core principles of course design. The first of these is to ensure client centricity, whilst maintaining an objectivity about the client and their goals; in other words to be simultaneously connected and objective. Secondly I would suggest that the course designer retains the delicate balance between client, sponsor and delivery agent.

Dr Joe Jaina (dictated on the weekend of his unexpected death).

Program director's experience

The initial clear and concise request for proposal came through the normal impersonal route. Far from "normal", however was the nature of the organization called "Stuart Milne Group". Naturally we discussed internally: "How can a regional, albeit successful, salt-of-the earth player afford business school fees for such an expansive and ambitious intervention?" SMG was always poised to surprise!

They engaged with us in discussion before our submission of the formal tender, took us objectively through the selection process and, having selected us, accepted not only the core program that their tender demanded but also an up-front strategy workshop he suggested to ensure that their development had an unambiguous focus – that of delivering their to-be-crafted six-year corporate strategic plan.

Humbled by the personal commitment that Stuart Milne, the man, was making and impacted by the magnitude of both the investment (circa 10 percent of prior year's profits) and the number of people attending the program (over 25 percent of the total employee pool), necessity was laid on us to be relevant and to make an impact. We had to leave a mark not a blur if we were going to add measurable value. Central to this was the program's intent: to cascade the core taught elements to each of the five managerial levels. This forced real creativity in our "teaching" techniques to meet participants, from the Group board to the factory floor, exactly where they were.

To ensure this, given the rapidity with which the whole population would complete this program (13 months), we agreed to have three program directors to accompany deliveries.[1]

Initial apprehension from many for whom it had been a long time since they'd entered an educational environment, especially from those who had not been to university, was quickly though not easily dispelled. From the start, participants were encouraged to make themselves known, to voice their opinions and engage in discussion. Exercises were interwoven to surprise, to open their minds. Laughter with, not at, others relaxed most into considering how they could approach familiar situations differently, as well as approaching different situations with the confidence of those who have begun to think from new angles.

CLH Rathbone

9.2 BNFL/Sellafield

A national major player; the world's most concentrated nuclear site

Continuous program run from 2003 to 2009.

*Program remit: To develop **commercial innovation leadership and accountable management** amongst executives, senior and middle managers in the midst of large-scale transformation.*

Background

By 2003 British Nuclear Fuels Ltd (BNFL) knew its nuclear sites would soon begin the process of closure. As part of this, BNFL prepared for permanent handover of all nuclear operations and sites.

During delivery of our first customized program, on 1 April 2005, British Nuclear Group (BNG) was registered as a new division of BNFL. Its task: to competitively bid for contracts to clean up nuclear sites whose ownership had on the same day been transferred to the newly created Nuclear Decommissioning Authority (NDA).

On 31 March 2007, BNG was disbanded. The NDA had decided to open competitive bidding for the management and operations of the sites exclusively to third parties.

BNFL continued, as did the existence of the nuclear sites. It is within those nuclear sites, and Sellafield in particular, that our development interventions unfolded.

Facts and figures

September 2003 to June 2004

Sellafield's top team completed the "Strategic Leadership", three-module program that revolved around the "process of leadership".[2] Further cohorts undertook an updated version of the same in 2005 and 2006.

September 2004

Reactor sites' top team started their version of the program, adapted to their specific, albeit similar, context.

February 2005

"Commercial Leadership" commenced for the senior manager population, mirroring and supporting the top team program.

February 2006

"Business Application Workshops" were launched to drive commercial practice through the appropriate contextualized application of tools that had been explored in the above programs.

August 2007

"Five Steps to Accountable Leadership" (5SAL) was created to equip Band 3 (middle) managers to be accountable for their remits, safely delivering to increasingly measurable performance targets, driving and responding to change, with impact and courage.

The business issues

In order to deal with the nation's aging nuclear installations, the UK government created the NDA (Nuclear Decommissioning Authority) on 1 April 2005. Its remit: to take ownership of all BNFL assets and liabilities and accelerate clean-up of nuclear waste. BNFL was forced to organize itself to competitively bid for contracts to manage UK sites that it had hitherto owned. If unsuccessful, it faced a new externally appointed top team. (By 2007, that alternative became a reality. On 24 November 2007, the existing executive board was replaced as one lot by that of the successful bidder, Nuclear Management Partnership

Limited-NMPL.[3] Only one executive, the last to be appointed by the previous incumbent, transferred over to the new top team.)

The executive team and senior managers faced a rapid transformation from an "owner-managed nuclear re-processing monopoly" to a "nuclear clean-up M&O contractor" operating in a competitive market place.

Management felt they had to:

- increase their shared commercial understanding and capability
- lead and accelerate transformational change
- position themselves to competitively retain the NDA contract.

Through an extensive tendering process, Cranfield School of Management was chosen as the executive development partner to help them achieve these aims. Through the six years that have ensued, we have worked passionately at a corporate and individual level to help the guardians of the world's most concentrated nuclear sites transform their conduct of operations to, with continuing safely, deliver increasingly visible and demanding results in their new commercial environment.

The approach

Consulting closely with the HR talent development team, members of the top team and representative operators across the group, we:

- designed what became a series of regularly updated modular interventions that include business simulations and implementation follow-up days
- led a team of over 20 faculty specialists
- program-directed each intervention to hold people accountable to deliver measurable benefits and to be able to synthesize key issues for the attention of the executive team
- created a series of 11 customized e-learning capsules to support the main subjects explored during the face-to-face sessions.

The program

The top and senior programs focused on the three bases of the process of leadership:

- setting direction
- aligning resources
- energizing others.

Superimposed upon these were the three stages of innovation: discontinuous, incremental and inter-organizational.

Covered in some detail were the following subjects:

- under "Setting direction": vision, mission, values, strategy, strategic assets, innovation and enterprise risk management
- under "Aligning resources": program and project management, finance, supply chain management and performance measurement
- under "Energizing others": leadership, change management and personal style.

This integrated development, designed through extensive one-to-one interviews and focus groups, encouraged immediate application to create a learning organization where, as iron sharpens iron, one individual sharpens another.

Following the above, the middle management program, 5SAL, focused on the two operational angles of leadership – alignment of resources and the energizing of others. The logic in this was that direction would be largely set by the executive and senior teams, and this in itself would be strongly influenced by the main customer: the NDA. Fundamentally informed by a training needs analysis, 5SAL builds the competencies to safely deliver whilst creating an environment of empowerment, within the context of continuous change, with impact and courage.

Making a difference

Within six months of completion of the executive and senior team programs, through participants' application of the concepts and tools explored during the sessions, Sellafield achieved 108 percent payback on their program investment. Within the equivalent post-program period, reactor sites had begun to roll out a root-and-branch approach to innovation within the individual sites. Even before completion, the second wave of Sellafield senior management programs yielded a tenfold payback from sustainable annualized savings that we were told could grow significantly when rolled-out across the entire site. Measured on the last program day (so as to ensure full participation), this level of payback appears to continue in the middle management 5SAL program.

Quote from the client sponsor

We have been through and are still facing a significant change in our organizational position. Cranfield joined our journey early in this process and were instrumental in helping to understand the learning gap in our senior management population.

Cranfield have not only kept pace with the level of change but in some cases were ahead. How many calls have I taken from Cora Lynn? "Lesley, have you seen the papers – it is as I expected ..."

In partnership each cohort delivered has been refreshed and updated in light of the latest organizational position. Feedback from the program has been excellent and there is evidence of significant cost savings across the business which can be attributed to certain aspects of the program.

I would have no hesitation in recommending Cranfield as a learning partner to any organization.

Lesley Bowen,
HR Manager – Head of Learning and Education

Key corporate sponsors

Barry Snelson, Sellafield MD 2003 to 2008; Lesley Bowen, Head of Learning and Education 2003 to present; the new NMPL Board.

Middle managers

Five steps to accountable leadership

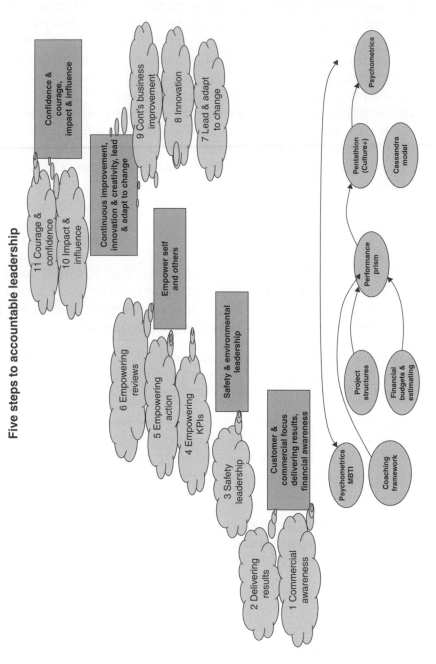

Program pictures

Top teams

Process of leadership

Strategy
Program output

- Strategic thinking
- Strategy implementation
- Innovation – continuous incremental improvement
- Cultural change

Leadership
Program inputs

- Leadership & management
- Team membership & effective delegation
- Incentivization & Motivation – Engaging troops
- Leadership obligations
- Communications & meetings
- Decision making, influence & persuasion

Commercial accountability
Program processes

- Program/project management ("Scope, Schedule, Cost")
- Financial awareness
- Customer focus & key account management
- Change & change management
- Bid process & management
- Performance measurement: safety, financial, contract outputs
- BU intradependency
- Alliance & supply chain management

Return on investment

Hardwired into the executive team and senior manager programs were half-day follow-up workshops to hold participants accountable for application of learning. In these sessions we were able to capture which tools and concepts learnt on the program were applied by participants in the context of their day-jobs. Some examples of applications include:

- **Program management disciplines**:
  – re-mobilized resources (eliminating multiple projects pursued in silo-isolation) using program management disciplines to a more sustainable business stream. Saved **£2m**.
- **Ishikawi (Fish bone)** – Used to identify aspects of the process that add or detract value. Conclusions were tested to see if

they can be applied as a generic solution to similar situations. "Pilot" results:
- revitalized capital equipment
- changed the process, eliminating major aspects and costs
- saved **£500k** to date
- *"could be saving billions if extended to other parts of the organization"* (executive board director, December 2005).
- **Performance measurement** (Performance prism) – Established and communicated realistic, achievable targets that concurrently meet organization's and stakeholders' needs:
  - focused on what delivers business benefits and specifically on what impacts on financial performance
  - reviewed the work of teams; agreed to eliminate one shift by deploying staff to more productive work in another part of the organization, replacing previous sub-contractors
  - savings assessed as **£2.5m** over next two or three years.
- **Stakeholder management in a major capital project** – Because of the "My minister is bigger than your minister" syndrome:
  - engaged upfront with the right people, including client stakeholders
  - renegotiated specific PBIs with customer
  - agreed in principle an incremental **£500k** fee.

Program components

1. Content – business school faculty.
2. Sellafield executives and senior managers as mentors.
3. Session introductions by executive team members.
4. Groupwork to drive pragmatic application within the different corporate units.
5. Tailored case studies to capture the corporate culture and recurring situations for study in the program sessions.
6. Tailored e-learning packages as a library to support learning before, during and after sessions.
7. Actor-led sessions to explore the parallels of project management with the history of Henry V.
8. Pre-program learning contract, positioning participants' skills relative to program content.

9. Pre-session prep work such as case studies and diagnostic questionnaires.
10. Business simulations to explore the interdependencies in BU strategic management.
11. Co-coaching at the end of each session to identify intended application and hold each other to account.
12. Experiential exercises to raise personal awareness and develop out-of-the-box thinking.
13. Learning log to personalize learning.
14. End-of-program capture of application to underscore and stimulate accountability to put learning into practice.
15. Post-program follow-up sessions to capture application of learning and extend learning networks.

Faculty experience

Why did I decide to work on this program in the first place?

I am passionate about using research to inform management practice but the processes of turning research into useable teaching materials and products can be challenging. I had been researching high-reliability organizations for a number of years but did not have the opportunity to teach this subject on the postgraduate or executive development programs.

Sellafield is an organization that operates in an extreme context. Most organizations that operate in high-hazard environments (Sellafield included) have policies and procedures in place to trap, avoid or mitigate serious untoward events but the focus is usually on either individual errors or technical faults. I was confident that a program that took a systems perspective and concentrated on the management, organizational and leadership aspects of safety/reliability would offer a unique angle. This has proven to be the case.

One of the most appealing aspects of this work was the opportunity to work on a program that had the potential for real business impact. I also wanted the opportunity to co-produce the program with Sellafield subject-matter experts. Combining academic theory, models and frameworks with Sellafield-specific inputs, examples and anecdotes has worked well.

Even though I knew that designing a program for Sellafield on safety leadership would be difficult, I did not hesitate to accept the offer to work on this program.

How did I engage at first with Sellafield?

Cora Lynn undertook an excellent needs assessment and she briefed me thoroughly. I was also given the names of key subject-matter experts. I spent several days at Sellafield to talk with a number of stakeholders about the program. On one occasion, the Head of Nuclear Safety pulled a team of eight people together to "grill" me! The first few meetings were a challenge but over time, I developed a relationship with these experts. The key for me was to make it clear that I was not there to tell them how to do safety but to co-produce and co-deliver a program that would provide an alternative perspective on safety and would have the potential to change attitudes and behavior.

What was my experience of delivering the sessions?

I have thoroughly enjoyed delivering the sessions. I have built a strong relationship with Bob Jones and Joe McClusky who co-deliver the sessions and we work well as a team. The mix of theory, activities and group discussion works well and the feedback has been positive. In the initial design of the program the Sellafield input was considerable, but over time Bob and Joe have taken more of a back seat, suggesting that they are confident that the Cranfield material and delivery works.

Although every session has the same content and format, each day is unique due to the inputs from the participants. We often have a good laugh with the groups, particularly with the group decision-making exercises.

What have I personally gained from the experience?

Working with Bob and Joe has been fantastic; they are great people. We constantly challenge each other and strive to improve the session. I have gained a great deal of confidence, particularly in teaching a subject to people who regard themselves as experts. I have also adapted some of the material for use in the health service.

Working with Sellafield has been an ideal opportunity to "field test" my research-based ideas, models and tools with a group of practitioners. I think that this is essential for a management researcher. Working with Sellafield has undoubtedly benefited my research. For example, Bob Jones wrote a letter of support for my successful application for an AIM Fellowship. He has also talked with the new directors to ensure that I can use Sellafield as a case study site.

Dr David Denyer

Program director's experience

This has been a rich, multi-layered partnership at a time of extreme transition. Ours was the privilege of being able to listen and challenge thinking as it emerged from the discussions in the face-to-face session. Groupwork presentations of tools and frameworks applied to their present and future options created rich discussions, expanded during off-line exchanges over coffee, lunch and dinner. This was the case across the layers – with the executive team, senior managers and middle managers. No questions were barred and no offence was taken as our sometimes "obvious", some would say academic, hypotheses were posed. The openness with which all participants explored even the most provocatively direct scenarios was testimony to the honesty with which the senior team and all those who followed wished to embrace the organizational and personal changes that their transformation demanded.

Our first challenge was to understand the scale of the required transformation and the technical/commercial implications of the same. Each nuclear site around the country presents it own unique issues as no two reactors are exactly the same. As for scale, the task facing Sellafield was and remains arguably the greatest.

In all sites, teams had to move from owner-managers to operations and maintenance providers, from experts in the reprocessing of spent fuel rods and the storage/guarding of nuclear waste to nuclear clean-up professionals, from process owners to project and program managers. It was insufficient for them to think of "doing things better"; "doing things differently" and "doing different things" had to be the quest. This, in a mission-critical organization, where error is simply intolerable, is tough. The failure-free culture flies in the face of innovation. Yet innovation is the only way to create the new organization that their situation demanded. Our role as Cranfield was to partner the teams, to equip them with frameworks that would help their thinking and with tools to test their options, to challenge and empower them on this journey.

From a scientific, safety-first, somewhat secretive organization (yet fully responsive to multiple stakeholders), funded on a "cost-plus" basis until as recently as 2003, Sellafield has evolved into a commercial entity, acutely aware of budgets, schedules, scope of work, of its necessity to deliver to contract without compromising safety, and proactive in its engagement with the community and broader stakeholders whose purposes it has to serve.

Significant business benefits gained from delivered programs testify to the participants' integrity and commitment to organizational development. The smooth transition to the new executive team speaks of a commercial ability to deal with extreme change.

CLH Rathbone

9.3 France Telecom Orange

A major multinational player

Continuous program run from 2004 to 2009.

Working collaboratively with France Telecom Orange's Corporate University and EM Lyon, we created and co-delivered a dynamic program for the **development of intrapreneurship**

The organization

After significant over-extension in what was largely acknowledged as industry-wide over-investment in 3G, France Telecom Orange delivered impressive recovery from near collapse. It stood in 2005 on the edge of renewed expansion, leveraging its Orange brand to increase its presence in the global mobile communications market. Concurrently, with a rich technology bank, France Telecom Orange aimed to seize opportunities and bring some of these ideas to market by developing home-bred intrapreneurs.

Facts and figures

Approximately 300 selected group talent from all France Telecom Orange subsidiaries, nationalities and business functions have completed an intensive two-center program. Core theme: "value creation". Aim: to build intrapreneurial talent across the functions, to develop an internal talent pool for potential multi-disciplined teams able to take France Telecom Orange's highly engineered possibilities to market realization.

The business issues

As a leader in today's dynamic, fast-paced, tight-margined communication industry, France Telecom Orange's challenges include the declining brand loyalty of a "pay-as-you-go" post-modern consumer. The company recognized a compelling need to differentiate its offering in what is largely a commoditized but investment-demanding market, in order to generate value from acquisitions and 3G investments.

To this end, France Telecom Orange sought to develop organic capability to turn home-grown inventions into revenue-generating services.

Reflecting its origins as France's national telephony provider and embracing the novel global platform its subsidiaries provide, France Telecom Orange chose as partners two business schools to mirror the multiculturalism.

The approach

It had to be seamless. EM Lyon and Cranfield joined forces to design and deliver a carefully blended modular program that includes:

- e-learning on finance
- team projects that culminate in a full, invention-specific business plan
- three one-week, face-to-face modules
- inter and intra-modular team coaching – through all phases of business plan development.

Delivered only in English at EM Lyon in France and Cranfield in the UK, the program, featuring Cranfield and EM Lyon faculty, builds integrated capability. Participants, "directed" in the first instance to "test" learning through their team projects, are encouraged to progressively apply new concepts within their individual areas of operation for enterprise-wide intrapreneurial development.

The program

Addresses four **core aspects** of **intrapreneurship**, namely:

- strategic innovation and project/program management for transformational implementation

- leadership and team management for purposeful, broad engagement
- finance and performance measurement for quantifiable results
- marketing and supply chain management for realization.

Additionally, the program occupies four "**intrapreneurial quadrants**" – reflecting what it takes to create value, what it takes to deliver and sustain:

- returns on investments
- market leadership
- operational efficiency and
- agile operations.

Three five-day, face-to-face sessions explore the core subjects and four quadrants of intrapreneurship (outlined above). Between sessions, participants pursue projects, working in their virtual teams to produce full business plans. These they present to a Group board member on the penultimate day of the last module. Individual and team feedback follows on the final program day. Shadowing the teams, a project coach validates submissions and guides them in the development of their propositions.

Making a difference

The program has:

- brought together future potential leaders from different Group subsidiaries (mostly acquisitions, largely since 2000)
- spotlighted the wealth of invention waiting within France Telecom Orange's research vaults for spirited innovation
- raised awareness of the multi-disciplined nature of intrapreneurship and the need for collaboration across the functions and divisions
- birthed new strategic networks
- skilled-up participants in the various aspects of business management – as applied to the concept of intrapreneurial value creation

- emphasized the importance of stakeholders, and the extent to which value, like beauty, lies in the eyes of the stakeholder.

Key corporate sponsors

Marie-Catherine Combe, FTO Project Leader, Stephane Voitrin, FTO Project Manager.

Program content

The program is an exploration of the factors that drive innovation and value. Focused on an intrapreneurial challenge set by the corporate Central Innovation Team, it starts with leadership, and specifically team leadership. Variations are considered as most teams now work remotely, over different time zones and with dotted and straight-line responsibilities which are seldom shared. The project is scoped by the teams, bound by self-imposed and agreed governance practices, roles and responsibilities.

Module 2 introduces the functional disciplines. Considered are the financial factors of risk and return over time, the marketing aspects of what benefits go to whom and how they are to be delivered, the supply chain and the relationships that govern its efficacy, and the performance measures that both guide activity and hold individuals to account.

Module 3 concludes with communication strategy, the process for integrating a strategic project into the existing structures of a major corporate and the winning presentation – in this program to a panel of three senior corporate players and the program director.

Tested are not only participants' ability to apply the learning to a real situation but even more emphatically their ability, as disparate individuals, to forge and work in an intrapreneurial team, over a period of six months, collaboratively, negotiating internally for information and resources, and resolving inter-personal conflict, despite distance and language barriers.

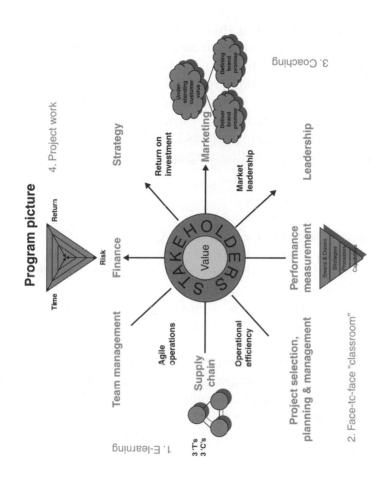

Program picture

Time · Return · Risk

Finance

4. Project work

Strategy

Return on investment

Marketing

Market leadership

Leadership

Team management

Agile operations

Supply chain

Operational efficiency

Project selection, planning & management

Performance measurement

STAKEHOLDERS

Value

Understanding customer value

Defining brand promise

Deliver brand promise

3. Coaching

2. Face-to-face "classroom"

1. E-learning

3 'T's
3 'C's

Swans & Owans
Strategies
'Processes'
Capabilities

Supporting this journey through all three modules are two distinct coaches – one for participants as individuals (an executive coach) and another (the project coach) to assist with progress on the program deliverable.

Return on investment

A fundamental feature of this program is the project that runs through each edition. To the selected project themes, participants are required to apply the learning (a first point of application) from the modules and to present their conclusions on the penultimate day of the third and final module. Overall, 17 innovation concepts have been explored by these selected Group talents. From these, four specific projects have been advanced to prototype and market exploration stages.

Program components

1. Content – business school faculty.
2. Senior panel to receive final project presentations.
3. Pre-modular questionnaires – connecting participants to each module.
4. Pre-modular prep work – case studies and relevant articles.
5. Project (cohort specific) as first point of application for learning.
6. E-learning to prepare participants for live sessions.
7. Coaching – two program directors, one as project coach and the second as executive coach.
8. Inter-modular team work to deliver project content.
9. Evening activities – team dinners, cohort dinners.
10. Follow-up debrief with program sponsor.

Faculty experience

At Cranfield, we aim to make a virtuous circle of academic research followed by practical application to test that research and finally classroom teaching to disseminate the learning and enable application. To exemplify, my work on Initial Public Offerings

(IPOs), and in particular state utilities, led me to supervise an Exec MBA student-project on BT's financial strategy. The student achieved the highest mark for his practical project on "Shareholder value at BT" and I was subsequently commissioned to work on aspects of "shareholder value" within the company. It was therefore natural for me to be very interested in working with another telecommunications company, especially France Telecom, as it was then known, given its leading European position, and to further my knowledge of the sector.

We take a team approach to client engagement and management at Cranfield. The team "leader" or client manager has a strong role to play. The Cranfield "team", the delegates and the client company management team form a three-way link where the informal "learning contract" between the parties has to work to make the program successful.

Our team leader and all the France Telecom Orange HR staff provided clear guidance on their expectations, giving me all the necessary info to make my contribution relevant and focused to France Telecom Orange.

The projects that participants had to work through provided clear links between our teaching of concepts and France Telecom Orange relevance. While of clear benefit to the participants, the various projects also gave me valuable insight into the inner workings of a large multinational telco, not only of their finances but also of their strategy, marketing and approach to customers.

Delivery of the program was challenging but very rewarding for a number of reasons:

1. The professional background of participants is very varied. It is not unusual to have an expert in finance as well as someone who had absolutely no financial skills in the same cohort. Our not-too-dissimilar experience of working with MBA classes helped but, unlike an MBA class, these participants are all experts on France Telecom Orange and the telco sector. By applying financial concepts in an interesting and relevant way to their management challenges, I aim to demonstrate the value of financial information. Examples from other companies and industries also help to focus their learning. My major contribution, however, is to harness the expertise that is in the class, and to help participants share it in a meaningful way, in order to catalyze learning and development.

2. *The different parts of France Telecom Orange rom which participants came added intrigue. It is important to recognize that although they are all from the same company, each of the unique entities from which participants come has its own sub-culture (i.e. TPSA, Mobinil, Jordan Telecom or Orange). To maintain participants' interest and give relevance, it is important to provide examples and anecdotes from their own entity. On the other hand, it is also very important to get them to recognize the corporate point of view and in particular the overall shareholder perspective. The challenge is to talk local but keep making the link to the Group.*

3. *Managing expectations has always been a challenge. Keeping right up to date with the latest issues faced by the company and the sector is very important for credibility. The current share price is a simple example but I also need to know what the latest analysts' report is saying, how the board or the investor relations department have reacted, and even what France Telecom Orange is using as the current internal rate for cost of capital to evaluate investments. Colleagues at France Telecom Orange and contacts in the industry outside France Telecom Orange have been of immense help.*

4. *The knowledge bank I have built up over the years has given me greater confidence and made my material of increasing relevance to the delegates. It is very rewarding to be able to explain a company-specific issue even though I am an "outsider".*

What did I gain from delivering on the program? The greatest reward comes when I finish the two-day marathon and get a cheer, a good review and words of appreciation. Apart from that, I also gain knowledge, satisfaction, fun and friends.

Sri Srikanthan

Program director's experience

Imagine working with a group of aficionados whose love affair you do not understand and barely share. That was my opening gambit with France Telecom Orange. Communication is truly vital. Yet I had to be forgiven many times over for thinking that the communication gadgets and their functionalities at the center of this fascination were merely a means to that very practical vitality.

What I lost in love for the "products" was compensated for by fascination with a full-on multicultural group of pulsating entre-preneurs. From the outer perimeters of the UK, France, Poland, Romania, Spain, Egypt, Senegal, Australia and Singapore, participants from more than 25 countries joined to create project teams that together explored potential new revenue streams.

This program highlighted many reasons why projects within development programs are wonderful and difficult.

1. How can participants complete projects to a high standard, given that they continue with their highly demanding day jobs whilst they handle totally new concepts?
2. How can they be challenged to apply the learning to their own day jobs when they are consumed with applying them to a project that has to be presented to an influential panel by the end of the full program?
3. How can you ensure that proposed projects are sufficiently strategic for the organization to commit resources to take them to commercial fruition after final presentation?
4. How do you continue to come up with viable project ideas that are sufficiently clear to raise the enthusiasm of intelligent participants?
5. How do you maintain enthusiasm for the projects if the members of the creative team disband to their individual remits after presentation?

It's a heady, fast-thinking and fast-action partnership with this international giant, punching with the best in the world of fast-moving electronic goods, knowing that life-cycles of products and services are as short as nine months and that end-users' expectations include falling unit costs and a constant stream of amusing, free-of-charge additional features!

CLH Rathbone

9.4 EDF

An international major player; the fifth largest global electricity producer

Continuous program run from 2004 to 2009.

Partnering with the EDF Corporate University to design and deliver **executive development to accelerate business transformation**

The Organization

EDF is the world's fifth-largest energy company and the premier global nuclear operator, with a fleet of 58 nuclear power stations supplying the bulk of its fully integrated provision. It also owns and operates coal and CCGT stations, hydroelectric plants, wind farms and solar panel installations, is spearheading development of biomass generation and fossil-fired plants and is building its stock of gas. Not surprisingly, its ambition includes being a major global player in the use of non-CO_2-emitting technology. The Group employs 159,000 people worldwide (January 2009), enjoys a global turnover approaching €60bn (2008) and is 85 percent owned by the French government. (Having been the national monopoly electricity supplier of France, an IPO was successfully concluded in 2006.) All EDF entities operate in a mixed framework of liberated and regulated competitive markets, with the exception of the UK market, which is fully deregulated.

The business

Through a bold strategy of targeted acquisitions, the latest and largest being the 2008 purchase of British Energy for £12.5bn, EDF has transformed itself from an exclusively French entity to an international concern. Its incorporated entities include EDF SA (France), EDF Energy (100 percent owned: UK), EnBW (45 percent owned: Germany) and Edison (50 percent owned: Italy). Beyond this, EDF has selective investments in Europe

(Poland, Hungary, Belgium, Austria, Slovakia, Switzerland, and Spain) as well as the United States, South Africa, China and Vietnam, leveraging its expertise as premier nuclear operators and engineers. Additionally, the Group's commitment to sustainability, energy security and carbon neutrality is underpinned by its development of alternative generation sources through its subsidiary, EDF Energies Nouvelles.

The development challenge

Initially, in 2004, as a capital-intensive operator, accelerated transformation and cohesion of the Group were viewed as essential for dealing with challenges created by:

- becoming an international/global "merit good" player[4]
- increasing competition in a deregulating French energy market
- the need to improve Group performance to provide for future needs.

In response to these challenges, the EDF Corporate University was established and Cranfield was chosen within a year of its inception as one of three founding business school partners.

Five years on, in August 2009, Cranfield continues to deliver and perennially update the program suite described below. The aim is to engage participants from EDF's diverse entities in focused exchanges, to give them an outside–in view of the four pillars of commercial reality (markets, strategy, people, performance), to expand their skills as highly educated leaders, and to drive learning into practice, partnering EDF in its escalating and increasingly impressive performance.

The approach

In partnership with executives from EDF's Corporate University and EDF operational subject experts, and collaborating with faculty from other business schools including London Business School, Insead and ESCP-EAP, Cranfield's Centre for

Customized Executive Development designed a suite of four interrelated programs, contextualized to EDF, that:

- provided provocative yet pragmatic content
- attracted participants from international subsidiaries, leveraging diversity and enhancing unity across the Group
- created a participative, safe learning environment – in a culture that is largely reflective, accustomed to formal teaching and structure
- challenged participants to translate commercial thinking into practice at their level of the business.

The partnership and suite of four programs has:

- contributed expertise on core transformational subjects (such as corporate social responsibility and brand innovation) to build shared awareness and competence throughout the three top management ranks, namely: talent, executives and senior executives
- established an EDF-funded research project to explore social and environmental responsibility across the European energy sector
- researched and delivered workshops to explore brand development and brand creation in light of the new commercial agenda
- developed a business case study that captures the creation of EnBW's new brand (Yello) in the electricity market of Germany.

Making a difference

The programs have:

- given momentum to a forward-looking and global dialogue
- raised open debate on strategic issues
- created new informal networks across functions, business units, subsidiaries and management layers in the wider Group
- grown the perception of EDF as an international group that includes cultures beyond that of France

- challenged mindsets and encouraged participants to do likewise
- successfully blended internal knowledge and experience from EDF with external expertise from Cranfield and other business schools.

Why Cranfield?

EDF's course on "Management Fundamentals" with Cranfield University has been a recurrent success for EDF corporate university all through these years. The unique Cranfield blend of cutting edge theory and constant focus on implementation has been at the core of the success. On top of that, the constant interaction with the program director Cora Lynn Heimer Rathbone, who has been a master in running and implementing the program, has added to the unique dimension of these four-pillar modules. It is part of our must-do for our young managers at EDF.

Dr David Jestaz,
Head of EDF Corporate University

Facts and figures

To date (January 2009) over 600 EDF managers and leaders from France, England, Germany, Italy, Poland and Hungary as well as Corsica, Guadeloupe and Martinique have attended the suite of four interconnected programs, designed in partnership with the EDF Corporate University to enhance future leaders' understanding of markets, strategy, people management and performance management within EDF. Programs are held at Cranfield in the UK and at the EDF Corporate University at Chatou, Paris.

Key corporate sponsors

Dr David Jestaz, Director of the EDF Corporate University; Jerome Gueugnier, Operations Director; Martine Zabner, Design

Director; Michel Marchand, original Director of Business School

EDF management fundamentals suite

EDF MARKETS An overview:	EDF STRATEGY An overview:	EDF PEOPLE An overview:	EDF PERF. An overview:
Big picture: market forces & parameters ⬇ Therefore: differentiation external chain B2B B2C	Big picture: Europe ⬇ Options: organic growth grafted-on growth something new	The formal organization ⬇ You ⬇ You in your organization ⬇ A living organization	Triangulation ⬇ Aspects of perf.: financial core business excellence social & environ. responsibility

Partnerships.

Program suite picture

Return on investment

EDF Corporate University has wanted to ensure that whilst participants on this suite of programs are recommended by their career managers, they self-select to attend. There is no expectation that they complete all four programs nor that they do so in the order described above. This has made it difficult to capture the application of the learning and therefore to measure benefits derived as a result.

Notwithstanding, many participants choose to attend all programs once they become aware of the suite. That must be evidence of the value they perceive in the program for themselves and their careers.

Program components

1. Content – business school faculty.
2. EDF expert and director contributions.
3. Groupwork and faculty surgeries to facilitate dialogue and explore application of learning across EDF's diverse entities.
4. Pre-session diagnostic and psychometric questionnaires to personalize the program to participants' realities.
5. Pre-modular prep work such as case studies and relevant articles.
6. E-learning to support the financial sessions.
7. Co-coaching and peer feedback.
8. Experiential exercises to provoke out-of-the-box thinking and raise personal awareness.
9. Business simulations – to give an experience of strategic BU management.
10. An EDF-specific case study to exemplify innovation.
11. Learning logs to capture and personalize learning.
12. Evening activities – cohort dinners.
13. Follow-up debrief with sponsors.
14. Follow-up exchanges with select participants.

Faculty experience

I was initially approached by Cora Lynn to teach on the EDF Strategy program in 2005. After a couple of spirited conversations with her, the content and form of the session was mutually agreed.

My field of expertise is M&A, and an interesting point of departure was my desire to base my input around a tried and tested case study drawn from a very different industry to the client's own. Gratifyingly this approach turned out to work very well, with participants able to experience an illustration of the major M&A issues free from any "industry insider" politics or bias.

How would I describe the experience of delivering the sessions? Dynamic! With participants drawn from both head office and the national operating companies, many with their recent acquisition by EDF still fresh in their minds, there was never a shortage of debate, particularly around how M&A integration should be handled. The pace and relevance increased still further in 2008 when the M&A session was delivered on the day EDF announced the acquisition of British Energy. Rewardingly for the quality of exchange, by March 2009 some of the British Energy managers were themselves participants on the program.

As well as being interesting in its own right, the EDF experience has turned out to be a useful proving ground for some of our developing M&A research themes, for example around value-creating corporate configurations.[5]

Dr Richard Schoenberg

Program director's experience

Working with this global leader has never ceased to stretch us as development providers.

Not only does EDF own the world's largest fleet of nuclear power stations, making it the premier global operator of nuclear plants, it was also, when we started working with them, fully owned by the French government. "Service publique" runs through its somewhat blue veins. Early on, towards the end of a "managing performance" session where we had been discussing shareholder value, one senior participant growled from the back of our U-shaped seating arrangement; "Cora Lynn, vous et moi, nous n'avons pas le meme sens de 'valeur'!".[6]

We had a lot to learn. Participants are extremely competent. They are also culturally very diverse – nationally, educationally, functionally and organizationally.

COMEX and the more senior ranks were populated largely by "Enarcs" and "Science Po" graduates. Many participants had scientific PhDs, often in nuclear physics or related disciplines. Highly educated and extremely well connected, most possess all the charm and engineering rigor imaginable of the French.

Partnering as a concept was extremely precise in the role we played. The Corporate University itself became a major change agent as it brought people from the different entities together to participate in our and other external providers' programs. The cross-cultural discussions that emerged were in themselves instrumental in the learning that occurred – on the part of participants and of ourselves as development providers.

With a change in French government came a change in leadership at EDF. That ushered in the IPO of 2006. We witnessed how the opportunity to personally own shares in EDF increased participants' interests in all things commercial. Enthusiasm to adopt and use the tools and techniques discussed in the sessions tangibly grew.

Working with the caliber and diversity of talent from EDF, often juggling up to six nationalities and more than four business entities in the same room, created a rich development dynamic that was uniquely and wholly theirs.

CLH Rathbone

9.5 L'Oréal

A global major player; the global leader in beauty products

9.5.1 L'Oréal TAM

Continuous program run from 2005 to 2009.

TAM (Transition to Advanced Management): Enabling manag-ers to make the **transition into heads of functions and members of management committees**

The organization

In 2004, L'Oréal, the world leader in the beauty business, was enjoying what (running up to 2007) amounted to 20 years of unbroken double-digit profit growth. Increasing internation-alization required managers to transition for the first time into heads of functions, and thus members of management committees, to grow their capability to deal with increasingly complex people management issues.

By 2009, nearly 900 managers from L'Oréal's business-unit management committee population had attended the five-day program, with up to 16 nationalities represented at any one event, drawn from across all five continents.

Delivered in English and French at Cranfield's Centre for Management Development, the program has been rolled out to other world regions, delivered by local business school providers.

The business issues

L'Oréal recruits the best from the best academic institutions, very occasionally cross-recruiting proven expertise from similarly profiled organizations. From a tradition that grows its own world-class leaders, MDC Europe (L'Oréal's in-house leadership development division) recognized that its rich provision for business education needed to be supplemented by management development to address the people-management needs of a crucial population of managers who would be managing other managers for the first time.

A second challenge for this population was how, as a member of a management committee, to represent one's function yet collaboratively contribute to the strategy of the business unit.

In partnership with Cranfield, MDC Europe has realized a program that equips high-powered high-achievers to evaluate their behaviors in order to be global "leaders of leaders" in dynamic, fast-moving, driven team environments.

The approach

The program needed to:

- capture the imagination of proven young professionals on the cusp of significant transition to a new level of responsibility
- be experiential to increase self-awareness for them to take ownership of their own behavioral development
- reflect the uniqueness of the L'Oréal culture
- embrace and leverage the national, functional and business unit diversity represented by groups of up to 30 at a time.

The co-created leadership journey started from four perspectives:

- competencies L'Oréal required of a member of a management committee
- motivations of individual participants: work values and communicated behaviors mapped against global dilemmas
- team management and their own authentic individual leadership journey
- behaviors that enable effective contribution to BU strategy.

The program

The five-day program blends French and Anglo-Saxon business school subject specialists with one-to-one coaches and L'Oréal contributing executives to work at the level of the:

- Individual – that which each participant naturally brings to their role and the personal challenges within that which encourage development of self and others.
- The group – each participant experiences what it takes to represent their function yet contribute to strategy in cross-national BU committees.
- The organization – such that each participant may better understand L'Oréal's expectations of them at this new and crucial level of business leadership.

This innovative program revolves around three "tools":

- the Spony Profile Model
- the myth of Percival and
- an IT-enabled FMCG business simulation.

Making a difference

The program has:

- given permission for discussions around different cultural work values and the need to match individual motivation to the roles people are asked to fulfill in order to achieve sustainable performance
- raised awareness of the importance of one's own behaviors – the need to take responsibility for the impact of such on others
- given birth to new strategic networks
- addressed the people-management challenges of management committee membership and responsibility
- created moments of deep reflection for increased maturity through greater self-awareness.

As for the real test of value, i.e. the effect the program has on participants returning to their "daily jobs", I recently spoke to one of our country general managers who expressed how pleasantly surprised he was to see the impact that the program had had on his marketing director [who came] back from the seminar a different person: more present, listening, sharing with his team and being noticeably less stressed ... in short a living example of "mission accomplished".

Victoria Wahlen, original Program Manager, L'Oréal

Key corporate sponsors

David Arnera, Patrick Lissmann, Celica Thellier.

Return on investment

With a history of high attrition, L'Oréal has been able to boast lower attrition from past participants than from others who have not attended TAM in that target population.

Program components

1. Content – business school faculty.
2. L'Oréal general manager and senior HR director contributions – to ground the program experience in L'Oréal's reality.
3. Pre-modular questionnaires – connecting participants to the session.
4. Tailored case studies to open the session with the type of L'Oréalian challenges that the program would address.
5. Actors to guide self-discovery and explore personal leadership journeys through the metaphor of Perceval.
6. Creative pieces to tap into deeper passion.
7. Coaching from one-to-one SPM feedback givers.[7]

TAM course content

How does it relate to what we have done so far?

- **Why this seminar?**

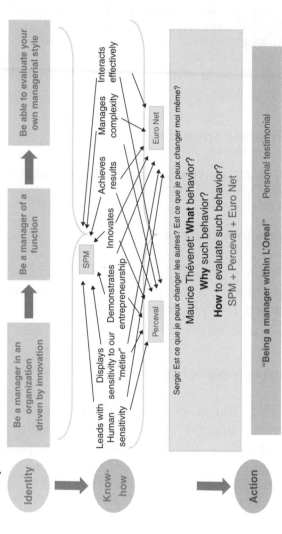

8. Guided peer feedback and peer coaching sessions.
9. Small group discussions to anchor learning in L'Oréal's reality.
10. Personal journal to encourage reflection and personalization of the learning.
11. Business simulation to trial new behaviors in a strategic and highly pressured L'Oréal-like environment.
12. Evening activities – team dinners and cohort dinner.
13. Follow-up debrief with individual faculty and program sponsor.
14. Follow-up exchanges with select participants.

Faculty experience

As the creator of SPM, I was very interested in the opportunity to use the model with a population of managers who are currently challenged in their work experience by the growing issue of understanding cultural differences and implementing that under-standing through the management of multicultural teams. The dedicated commitment of both L'Oréal's program managers and Cranfield (through Cora Lynn Heimer Rathbone, Bill Wright and Capucine Carrier) convinced me that time and reflection would be given unsparingly to design and deliver a program to genuinely help L'Oréal directors become more effective global leaders. As an example, L'Oréal did not hesitate to endorse the cost of a one-to-one session feedback for each of their managers so that each participant could share and discuss the personal implication of their SPM results with an SPM expert.

The program has now been running for about five years and, taking a step back, it has been a great experience for me. Two main aspects should be highlighted:

- *The progressive integration of the knowledge and philosophy of SPM with the other sections of the seminar:*

  All the teaching members of the different parts of this seminar spent some time attending an SPM session and, conversely,

I attended all the other parts of the program. We were determined to share our knowledge in order to refine and integrate the different parts of this one-week seminar. I think this is a crucial step for providing participants with the feeling of joined-up understanding which will greatly help their personal development.

- *The refinement of the content/shape of the SPM session itself through a continuous discussion with the L'Oréal program managers and Cora Lynn, Bill and Capucine:*

We spent a huge amount of time reflecting on feedback from the participants and the impressions we built up while running the program so as to systematically challenge ourselves and refine our delivery. This was done in a very positive spirit with the sole purpose of increasing the quality of understanding of the participants. I sincerely felt that everybody was fully committed to pursue this quest. This approach is still ongoing and it is a never-ending process.

So for me this seminar remains a very good example of how to design a well-integrated management development program and I am very satisfied that SPM plays an important role in it.

Dr Gilles Spony

Program director's experience

Of all the programs I've had the pleasure to design and deliver whilst at Cranfield, this one must stand as the most creative and daring in the face of hard reason and commercial reality. L'Oréal has had a history of 20 years of double-digit growth. Success as global leaders in beauty gave them a confidence and aura that challenged our own. Yet we connected as cultures from the first meeting. David Arnera, Group Director of Management Development, proclaimed as he arrived in late 2004 at our Management Development Centre: "I can see that you are in touch with your bricks! Wonderful."

From the process of designing the program by meeting with over 100 L'Oréalians, through the corralling of an eclectic mix of subject experts and actors for the 15-strong delivery team to the actual delivery of each program with its 14-hour days for up to 16 different nationalities at a time, this program more than any other demands total engagement. It has been a humbling experience to see partici-pants, experienced directors, surprised by what they discover about themselves, begin to think differently about their behaviors and how they interact with others, become more committed to L'Oréal and prepared to champion, in their own way and in a manner acceptable within their national cultural norms, new competencies at their level of the organization.

CLH Rathbone

9.5.2 L'Oréal CMS

CMS (Country Manager Seminar)

*Enabling senior directors to **transition to the role of country managers (MDs)***

To date, since 2007, two CMS sessions have run, delivered once per annum for up to 15 new country managers at a time.

The business issue: Promotion to country managers requires L'Oréalians not only to (a) grow the business, (b) create a great place in which to work, and (c) be responsible corporate citizens, but also for the first time (d) to take charge of shared resources (i.e. manufacturing plant, R&D), and (e) to manage the entire business across all four divisions.

The approach

Working with Tony Russell, the Global Director for Senior Executive Development, we designed a program whose content covers Jean-Paul Agon's (CEO of L'Oréal since 2006) three corporate objectives (grow the business, create a great place in which to work, be responsible corporate citizens in the countries where we operate). We created an environment that starts and ends with the participants themselves. To start, each sets out their "stall", their personal business challenges, and drafts a core mission/vision statement. This begins the cross-fertilization that allows participants to inform each other on issues surrounding the management of shared resources and the complexity of leading across all four Group divisions within the dynamics of their specific country. On the final day, each defines their commitment to action by delineating their governance diaries, key milestones for their annual calendar. Given the importance of internal networks, and as a red thread through the five days, participants work in pairs and triads for the final 90 minutes of each day, applying the tools explored during the delivery day to their own reality, summarized in a business scenario that they submitted before arriving for the session.

The program

The five-day format consists of a series of half-days. In each half-day we present and explore a pragmatic tool or framework that structures thinking and discussion around one of Jean-Paul Agon's three corporate objectives. Each morning resumes with a synthesis of the application of the prior day's content into the participants' reality capturing the actual learning that emerged from the prior day. Through the daily process of faculty presentation, participant exploration, small-group application into a L'Oréalian generic case study, debrief of the same with peers and subject-experts, closer application in pairs and triads to more specific participant-centered situations and final individual reflection at the end of the day, we weave together a flexible, made-to-measure, purposeful toolkit for L'Oréal's top leaders and role models.

Content

For growing the business

Organic growth through (i) development of an explicit mission/vision statement, (ii) identification and leveraging of strategic assets to achieve that mission, in the context of (iii) strategic organizational configurations.

Innovation through the fivefold focus on (i) innovation strategy, within (ii) an innovation culture that generates (iii) ideas, sieved through (iv) clear selection criteria for (v) structured implementation.

For creating a great place to work

Greater insight into own leadership style gained through (i) a customized 360° and (ii) two psychometric tools followed by exploration of (iii) team constructs and what it takes to (iv) develop high-performance teams.

For being a responsible corporate citizen

(i) Identification of major stakeholders, (ii) mapping of their wants and requirements and (iii) possible strategies to be deployed.

Underpinning this thought stream are the co-coaching pairs that work together through each of the days.

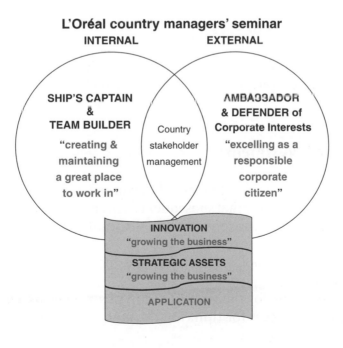

L'Oréal country managers' seminar

INTERNAL　　　　　EXTERNAL

SHIP'S CAPTAIN & TEAM BUILDER

"creating & maintaining a great place to work in"

Country stakeholder management

AMBASSADOR & DEFENDER of Corporate Interests

"excelling as a responsible corporate citizen"

INNOVATION
"growing the business"

STRATEGIC ASSETS
"growing the business"

APPLICATION

Making a difference

The program endeavored to

1. Equip L'Oréal's brightest leaders to be authentic national role models of the global enterprise.
2. Build a social support network of country managers who share a similar toolkit for the development of their country operations.
3. Create a safe environment for what are often young high-flyers to share their issues, not only business but also personal, and to invite peer support beyond the session.
4. Broaden participants' understanding of the Group, the global challenges it faces and the agendas to which they must individually and collectively contribute.
5. Empower them to use analytical tools and frameworks to structure their thinking and actions.
6. Enable participants to have a fresh look at their own leadership style. Beyond their technical brilliance, how can they build the balanced confidence that will allow them to better engage with others in order to empower growth through what is a highly organic, people-centric organization?

Key corporate sponsors

Tony Russell, Global Director of Senior Executive Development; Philippe Louvet, Global Group Director of Learning for Development.

Return on investment

Though we have no measurement of the return on investment from this program, we know that subsequent to the program participants have used the following tools with their Country teams:

• mission/vision tool to cohere the country management committee
• causal mapping for the identification of strategic assets
• innovation process for thinking through proactive creativity

- stakeholder mapping for identification and management of known stakeholders
- continuation of the co-coaching pairs through regular phone exchanges beyond the program's conclusion for mutual sustainable support.

Program components

1. Content – business school faculty.
2. L'Oréal COMEX contribution.
3. Pre-modular questionnaire to connect participants to the session.
4. 360° and psychometric to personalize the leadership components.
5. Pre-modular prep work, including relevant articles.
6. Co-coaching and triad work to encourage personal reflection and structured networking.
7. Learning log to encourage reflection and action planning.
8. Groupwork to hone the use of the tools and structure ways to apply them in the country COMEX structure.
9. Strong distance-learning element to extend the learning experience and drive relevant application.
10. Evening activities, including cohort dinner.
11. Follow-up debrief with program sponsor.

Faculty experience

L'Oréal's CEO Jean-Paul Agon has said that he wants his country managers to be "ambassadors" for L'Oréal. The company has made sustainable development one of its core business goals. It is crucial, therefore, that the country managers understand what sustainable development means for L'Oréal and how to explain this to internal and external stakeholders.

In order to familiarize myself with how the company sees the various issues, I spent a day in the global HQ in Paris with a number of staff, including the company's Chief Ethics Officer, the Head of Crisis-Management and the Director for Sustainable

Development. I also held extended telephone conversations with a couple of experienced country managers and, whilst traveling for Cranfield anyway, took the opportunity to spend time with a newly appointed L'Oréal country manager in Denmark, to understand his in-tray.

Even so, as a newcomer to the world of business schools (after a 30-year career as a campaigner and social entrepreneur) it was challenging for me to teach a roomful of new L'Oréal country managers, some operating in advanced markets, some in just-emerging markets. Stimulated by the initial exposure, I was able to develop my own learning and share that with many of our MBA students. When we visited China recently for the MBA International Business Experience, we visited L'Oréal's Chinese HQ in Shanghai for an excellent presentation on what is L'Oréal's fastest-growing market – and is already their second biggest. This was a valuable experience for our MBAs – but will also help me on my future work with L'Oréal because the insights need to be constantly refined and updated. As a global business with global principles and policies, L'Oréal, for me, is a great example of the challenges facing country managers in such companies: what has to be adopted, what can be adapted or ignored, and where to innovate "in-country" ahead of global policies being formulated.

Professor David Grayson, CBE

Program director's experience

It was very exciting first to be sounded out and then to receive this second commission from L'Oréal, particularly as it was for a very senior population, two levels above that of the TAM program and two below Group COMEX. Our opportunity to synergize messages and build upon Jean-Paul Agon's three key objectives – to grow the business, to create a great place to work in, and to be responsible corporate citizens – made sense as a "next step" to follow TAM.

Leveraging what we knew of this very organic organization and working very closely with the Global Director of Senior Executive Development, we realized that this program would have to be much more concrete than TAM. The pragmatism of bottom-line quarterly reporting demanded clear tools, limited to one per half-day, to ensure that the relevance of their application was tested within the week at Cranfield.

Clearly, participants were dynamic, entrepreneurial folk, many quite young for their responsibilities, taking significant personal risks by transplanting young families to new corners of the world. Thus the loneliness of leadership was not voiced but felt as each, at the start of the week. laid out the current state of their businesses and then the personal challenges those situations posed for them. A major by-product was therefore the creation of a resource network within each cohort such that participants could support each other not only during but more importantly beyond the program. Through co-coaching pairs and triads we saw individuals enter into honest and feisty exchanges. Some of these pairs and triads continue even two years after the first iteration, speaking of the value they provide well beyond the session itself.

It has been rewarding to hear about the tools and frameworks that participants have taken back and applied in their contexts. Stories from TAM participants who report in to country MDs who have attended CMS don't exactly give us quantifiables for return on investment calculations but they speak of an organization in whose holistic development we play a part.

CLH Rathbone

9.5.3 L'Oréal SCA

SCA (Strategic Change Architects)

Equipping human resource directors to be **strategic change architects**

Four versions ran in 2009.

The approach

Building on the five stages of strategy development, the program explores a series of interrelated tools to equip human resource directors to lead, map and manage the delivery of major change. To ensure relevance, we use composite L'Oréalian cases built from change scenarios that we ask participants to submit in advance of the session. These become the first point of application of each day's tool. At certain junctions of the week we invite participants to select their own scenario and to work on that in small groups to test application of the tools on more specific and unfabricated change situations. Each day concludes with participants in triads, using process consulting to surface concerns that linger over the relevance or use of the tools. This exercise at the end of each day also serves to gain commitment to action and to strengthen support structures beyond the program. Morning reflections over breakfast are presented back to the group by the participants themselves, and related to key questions that repeat throughout the week.

The Program

A five-day intervention, each day consecutively tackles one of the following questions:

1. What is the destination – your vision/mission, the end result that the change endeavors to deliver?
2. What are you likely to achieve doing nothing significantly differently – given the changes already in motion, the strategies already in place?
3. What strategies/changes do you need to introduce to achieve that which you are tasked to deliver – detailing the parts of the organization that need to change to deliver measurable benefits, the actual changes those parts of the organization need to undertake, the networks and stakeholders whose support you need to elicit to make those changes possible, and the infrastructure you need to put into place to sustain the change effort for fruition?
4. How do you make this happen? What are the influencing and project management tactics required by the change portfolio if you are to collectively deliver the envisaged result?
5. How do you consult through the change process to ensure you and others stay on track? What can you do to ensure that

the key change tactics are implemented and actually deliver the desired benefits? How do you hold each other accountable for delivering on promises, and holistically engage all to play their individual parts in a dynamic change process?

Making a difference

The program pragmatically builds the toolkit for change. It provides one, or at most two, tools per day with which human resource directors can facilitate the:

- setting of a clear, relevant (HR) vision to deliver the business strategy
- diagnosis of the organization: the "as is", the "to be" and the identification of the strategic (organizational) gap
- design and management of change programs
- overseeing and management of change projects
- holistic debriefing of change through strong, confident consultation around the process.

Participants' post-program quotes

"...Thank you again for the outstanding quality of the program in Cranfield! The topics of change and organizational design are absolutely critical at this time and I felt I learned a lot and can bring back real tools and strategies to the [team]. I was also impressed by the caliber of the HR team you had assembled from all countries and realize that despite coming from very different nationalities, generations and cultures they all shared in common the L'Oréal values and vision of HR. This training was also a fantastic human experience."

"I took the afternoon yesterday to brainstorm with my team who work on the project and presented them with the methodology (I focused on Cassandra, Kaleidoscope and the triangle of strategic challenge and, last but not least, process consulting).[8] It has been a rich and inspiring afternoon – we will definitely adopt the methodology. I will let you know how it works in practice in

this 'unstructured' world. Anyway, you already have some very interested clients for the future – the internal informal network is already working."

Key corporate sponsors

David Arnera, Global Director of Management Development, Marianne Pennannauch, Head of HR Reruitment and Development, Richard Humphreys, Group Director of HR Community.

Content

Strategic assets and organizational configurations, talent management, process consulting, mission/vision, change kaleidoscope, Cassandra, change process (AITA), project management, change triangle and boxes.

Return on investment

One participant engaged her entire team in the process of applying the tools to a set of defined change challenges on an "away day". Another escalated the process to Group level and used it to agree and map the approach they would collectively take to manage a major change initiative with clearly defined, measurable benefits.

Program components

1. Content – business school faculty.
2. Senior director introduction and contextual presentation.
3. Pre-modular questionnaires to connect participants to each module.
4. Participant scenario to focus on core change challenge.
5. Learning logs to personalize learning.
6. Groupwork to drive the practice of the tools as applied to selected scenarios.

SCA course content

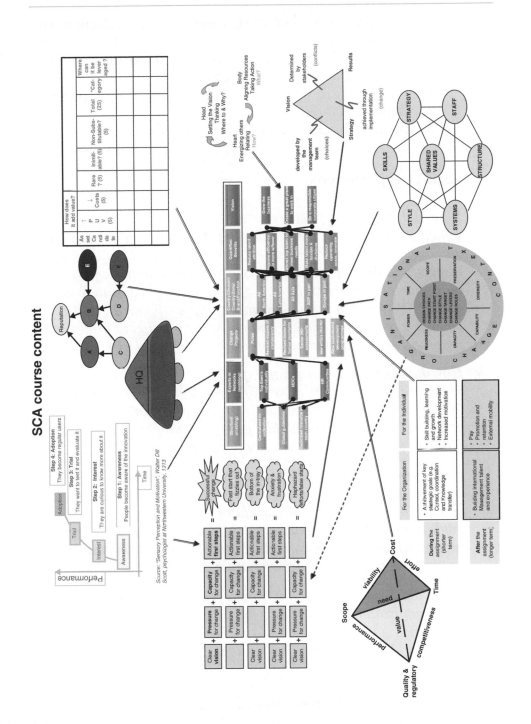

Source: "Sensory Perception and Motivation", Walter Dill Scott, psychologist at Northwestern University, 1313

7. Co-coaching and triad work to encourage reflection and appreciative enquiry.
8. Evening and breakfast activities – to build deep support networks and accountability webs.
9. Follow-up email, phone and live exchanges with program participants.
10. Milestone debriefs with program sponsors.

Faculty experience

Why did I engage? Well, you asked me! And I guess this is something to do with the relationship between you as consultant and me as faculty. You asked, and I agreed, (a) because I respect you and the enormous energy and commitment you put into your role as consultant, (b) I have worked with you and L'Oréal before and it was an interesting assignment, and (c) if you are running the show I know it will be a highly professional program, which I would be happy to be associated with.

How did I engage? We met, you explained the purpose and structure of the program, and the nature of the delegates. I already knew a fair bit about the organization from the previous program. This prior knowledge was invaluable, given the rather unique culture of L'Oréal, and in particular the organization structure.

I presented a session which focused on the inimitable and valuable strategic assets of the L'Oréal; I got them to "audit" the asset base of their own part of the organization, and to share and discuss implications. We also addressed asset-creating corporate configurations, which if I recall correctly provoked some interesting debate about the appropriate configuration for L'Oréal.

What did I gain? When one works with senior executives from any organization you have two major ways of learning from this experience: (1) you get to find out whether your ideas, theories, frameworks are any damn use to them! And (2) you learn fascinating insights into their "practice". When we put these two things together we are able to adjust and adapt our ideas and theories, and occasionally an issue gets raised that provokes questions that you have never considered before. This can prompt thoughts and *explorations that may result in new thinking. These are the real pay-offs from having the chance to interact with senior practitioners.*

Professor Cliff Bowman

Program director's experience

This third program represented a particular challenge for us as development partners. The original remit – to build, in a one-week residential session, business partner and change management skills in the HR population – had been addressed in each of the two prior years, but not to the satisfaction of L'Oréal. Therefore the commissioning team re-tendered with a narrower brief – to only develop change management skills.

Knowing L'Oréal and the internal positioning of the HR population, we were reluctant to build in them what might ultimately only be seen as an operational capability.

Through heated discussion, we agreed to equip HR professionals to manage change as strategic change architects. Wording was, always is, important. It was not sufficient to equip participants to map and manage-to-delivery significant change programs. More importantly, particularly if the change did not originate with them, the session needed to up-skill participants to partner the commissioning business leaders (general managers, country MDs, senior executives) in the specification of the change: its purpose and quantifiable benefits, the alternatives to the proposed change, its stakeholders and the implications of the undertaking.

Together we built a highly reflective action-learning program. During the delivery, with three very senior commissioning sponsors at the back of the room through the full duration of the week, the level of engagement we attained from participants, themselves a very senior group of human resource directors, was outstanding. Complexity was heightened by the fact that one participant was our prime commissioner for TAM, another had been a participant on one of the prior disappointing change management programs and had not wanted to attend, a third was responsible for all training and development for L'Oréal USA and a fourth was the equivalent for L'Oréal Latin America. Not quite "teaching your grandmother to suck eggs" but the sentiments were not dissimilar before the session began.

We learnt to work hand-in-glove with professionals who understood our trade, who nevertheless willingly participated. Like a stone thrown into a pond, the program has sent ripples that spread extensively. Among other lessons, we've learnt to condense and spin-off shorter versions: a half-day master class, a one-day team session, a two-day workshop. A series of project-specific options to the one-week session have been effectively delivered: a half-day one-to-one master class for senior players, a one-day workshop for a BU team, and a two-day workshop for a zone top-team.

Two key lessons rise to the top of what for us as a delivery team has been a great learning experience: (1) work with the client's complexity as you know it to be and, with that, (2) have the courage to propose and defend a "best case" or to walk away from a commission if the development scope will not serve the population in question.

CLH Rathbone

9.6   Oracle

A global giant; THE global information company

Program runs from 2007 to 2009.

*Supporting Oracle's key talents to become active **drivers of strategy** **and agents of change within their teams***

The organization

Oracle is arguably *the* global information company. World leaders in database and middleware, through an aggressive strategy of consecutive acquisitions of such names as Siebel, PeopleSoft, Hyperion and Sun Microsystems,[9] the corporate has also become a global one-stop-shop for IT business applications. This program explicitly commissioned by the EMEA Senior Vice President of Operations exists to develop Oracle's future leaders. The target: a population of high-performing, highly competitive, internationally minded directors and senior directors.

Facts and figures

Two cohorts of 30 participants have completed the three-module, three-venue program. The third iteration in three years was set to start in November 2009. Module 1 takes place in Barcelona, Spain, and is delivered by our partner, IESE Business School. Module 2 runs at the IEDC Business School in Bled, Slovenia, with content shared between IESE and Cranfield. Module 3 concludes at Cranfield School of Management, England.

The business issues

Operating in a fast-moving, highly competitive global arena, vying against known database, middleware and applications giants such as IBM, Microsoft and SAP, Oracle needs to retain its position as the technology pace-setter. Successful leaders in

Oracle must therefore not just deliver continuing double-digit growth of existing business and EBIT margins approaching 50 percent, but also carve out new business opportunities, almost always led by the acquisition of emerging-technology companies, and integrate those acquisitions from which the new technologies arise. The speed with which decisions are taken in what is a surprisingly centralized and highly networked organization is exemplified by the acquisition of Sun Microsystems. Announced on 20 April 2009, the deal was started and closed within ten days by the triumvirate of Ellison, Phillips and Catz. This was against the backdrop of stalled negotiations that had been going on for as many months between IBM and Sun. Truly brave, amazing and admirable. Developing leaders for the future of a corporate that creates the future is no mean feat for any executive development organization.

The approach

An independent needs assessment was summarized in a Request for Proposal to which eight top European business schools were invited to respond. Cranfield, in partnership with IESE, won the bidding process. The "Oracle Executive Management Program for High Potentials" was renamed "4Sight", and a single annual run offered "by invitation only" to roughly 30 selected managers across the EMEA region was agreed.

Through a series of focus groups composed of senior vice presidents and possible participants, the objectives for 4Sight were refined and the content and process was sculpted to:

1. Broaden knowledge and understanding of the IT industry, the global environment and its trends.
2. Deepen understanding of Oracle's strategy, how things get done, how the lines of business work together, how to align resources, why Oracle is structured as it is (verticals, matrix).
3. Develop ability to lead teams, drive change and energize self and others.

Each of these objectives became the respective focus of Modules 1, 2 and 3.

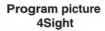

Program picture
4Sight

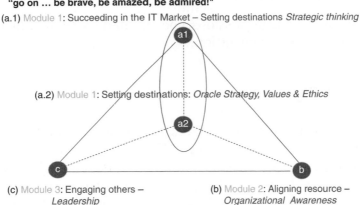

Executive development for talent
"go on ... be brave, be amazed, be admired!"

(a.1) Module 1: Succeeding in the IT Market – Setting destinations *Strategic thinking*

(a.2) Module 1: Setting destinations: *Oracle Strategy, Values & Ethics*

(c) Module 3: Engaging others – *Leadership*

(b) Module 2: Aligning resource – *Organizational Awareness*

The program

In brief, through a blend of content, group exercises, experiential activity and one-to-ones plus group video work, each respective module delivers and builds as outlined below.

Module I: Objectives

To broaden participants' perspective through the analysis of global trends, forcing reflection on the dynamics shaping business generally and the IT industry in particular in order to consider how possible changes (market, competitive, legislative or other) may influence Oracle's future performance and strategic direction.

Content: economic forces, value chain, innovation pelaton,[10] corporate responsibilities.

Module II: Objectives

Following on from the wider environmental issues of Module I and realizing the centricity of "the customer" in Oracles' value proposition, the second of the three modules explores "what it takes" to satisfy client demands (current and future): i.e. instigation of and adaptation to change, an "operational" process for innovation and an ability to "work at the intersection of the matrix".

Content: managing by missions, change management, innovation pentathlon,[11] value realization.

Module III: Objectives

In this final module participants are invited to look afresh at their personal leadership styles. This starts by exploring personal values and the influence of culture, benchmarked against factors that contribute to "exemplary performance". From this we proceed to map "owned" performance metrics. Referencing that, participants are invited to structure their intentions for authentic, integrated application of learning.

Content: SPM for national diversity, talent expectations, performance prism, authenticity.

Program flow

Each day's content is led by one academic faculty and connected to Oracle's reality through the contribution of an Oracle senior vice president (SVP). The team of 12 contributing Oracle SVPs, the "Oracle faculty", also engage with their respective academic faculty in advance of the session to ensure that the content and emphasis of the taught sessions are relevant to Oracle's evolving reality.

Additional to the content detailed above, this program benefits from a series of one-to-one video interviews and videoed syndicate work. These capture something of the participants' experience of the program and hold them to account, if only to themselves, for applying the learning in their contexts. The videos also provide observable data for coaching and peer feedback. Rarely do we see ourselves "in action". The self-reflection that these videos provide for participants to conduct their own analysis, to extend their self-awareness, is enormously valuable.

Program flow

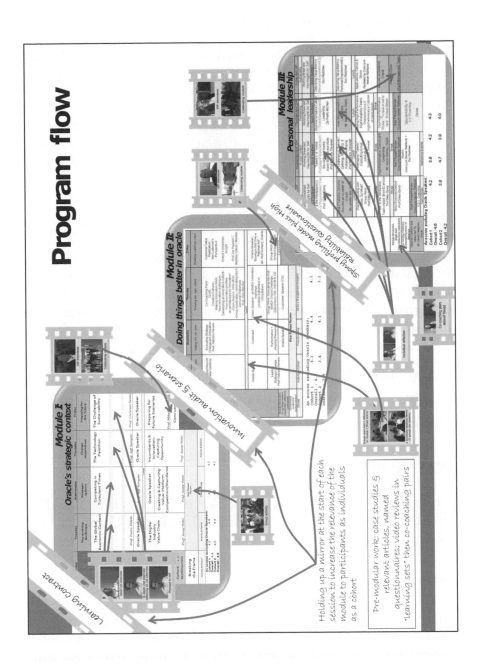

Module I — Oracle's strategic context

Module II — Doing things better in oracle

Module III — Personal leadership

Learning contract

Innovation audit & scenario

Group profiling model plus HIGH relationship questionnaire

Coaching plan stored thread

Individual reflection

Holding up a mirror at the start of each session to increase the relevance of the module to participants as individuals as a cohort

Pre-modular work: case studies & relevant articles, named questionnaires; video reviews in "learning sets" then co-coaching pairs

Making a difference

A quote from one of the contributing senior vice presidents:

"I enjoyed the day in Bled very much. Stimulated by the group and the presenters, I have created a new vision/mission/target for my business. Furthermore, my team and I decided to consequentially go down the road of value selling. I have asked Monika, who is heading our Insight Team, to contact [Professor] Joe. Perhaps he can help us to become 'masters in value selling'. Therefore I hope my stay in Bled was a win–win story. It was at least a win for me."

Some participant quotes:

*"I just wanted to say a huge thank you for a wonderful experience on the 4Sight program. You have done a fantastic job crafting the shape of this with everyone involved. I have got an enormous amount from this and am really excited about the journey, my personal journey ahead in the company that WILL be the **ipod experience for the enterprise software marketplace**. There are so many learnings, tools and techniques I am going to leverage from this experience. Here is to the journey ahead, hopefully a hero's journey."* David

"Many, many thanks for great experience." Irek

"Module 1 – great, Module 2 – [needs to be] more related to Oracle, Module 3 – excellent." Mattias

Key corporate sponsors

Sergio Giacoletto (instigator) prior SVP operations EMEA, Aline Tingstroem, senior consultant OTD EMEA, Loic le Guisquet, new SVP operations EMEA.

Return on investment

With two iterations of the program now completed, several individuals have been promoted within one year of program conclusion. Others have taken specific tools explored during the program and applied them in their specific area of responsibility to significant effect. Example: one participant combined his experience of the video elements and applied the principles of innovation and performance management to create a series of customer video interviews called "The Voice of the Customer". These will be displayed at HQ as testimonials of customer satisfaction. Three other participants worked with the specific faculty expert to integrate into Oracle's internal systems a toolkit for tracking and measuring the customer's ability to realize value from investment in Oracle solutions.

Program components

1. Content – business school faculty.
2. Oracle SVP contributions.
3. Pre-modular questionnaires to connect participants to each module.
4. Pre-modular prep work such as case studies and relevant articles.
5. Pre-program development tool to benchmark leadership behaviors against global dilemmas.
6. Pre-program webinars to brief participants and their managers.
7. Video of one-to-ones + syndicate sessions.
8. Business simulation to explore change tactics.
9. Creative sessions to open thinking.
10. Coaching from SPM experts in Module 3.
11. Co-coaching and inter-modular peer feedback on videos.
12. Learning log to encourage reflection and appropriation of learning.
13. End of program capture of application to underscore accountability.
14. Evening activities – treasure hunt, team dinners and bicycle ride in Barcelona; musicians and artist, Castle dinner and boat ride in Bled; dinner challenge, mask making and Airkix in Cranfield.
15. Follow-up review meeting with delivery partners.
16. Follow-up debrief with program sponsors.
17. Follow-up one-to-ones with select participants.

Faculty experience

When asked if I would like to work with Oracle I was extremely interested, given that my commercial background is in the IT industry. Having worked with Oracle on a commercial footing before, I was aware of their unique culture and regarded the teaching as a challenge as well as an opportunity to influence.

The teaching on strategic implementation and performance management was shared with a senior executive within Oracle. We spoke at length before the course to ensure that our messages were consistent and that my material was suitable for an Oracle audience.

With such a formidable new client I approached the teaching with some trepidation. However, the audience was very engaging and eager to learn and contribute to the class. Oracle is an extremely forceful organization within the IT industry and I enjoyed re-engaging with the business in such a dynamic and challenging way. I hope I gave participants something to think about and a way to approach their next strategic implementation.

Dr Dina Gray, visiting fellow; August 2009

Program director's experience

Following two years of round-table discussions around the topic of executive development in the context of a global player, a partnership of two business schools and one video-production organization was appointed. We were asked to design a high-impact program that would be brave, amazing and admired. Not an easy task given Oracle's panache and dominance over information management.

After two iterations, having had the pleasure of supporting and being supported by the contribution of 12 senior vice presidents, with delivery from over 12 academic faculty in three significant European business school venues, this program more than any other taught us the reality of collaboration. Beyond coordination in the allocation of program components on the basis of expertise and experience, beyond cooperation, where we share the stage to weave together a compelling and clear storyline, collaboration remains our goal as delivery partners. Despite strong mutual respect, natural competitive positions and different operating models make for creative tension. Yet this has proven to be of great benefit to the client as each business school strives to break creative boundaries in its individual delivery.

For what binds us as delivery partners is the passion for the client, passion for the rich depth of individual participants from up to 20 different countries per cohort. To this we bring our individual determination to fulfill the trust placed on us by the commission sponsors, backed by the excitement of an ambitious program that has more features and complex interplay than most programs we have seen, read about or had the pleasure of designing and delivering.

CLH Rathbone

Conclusion

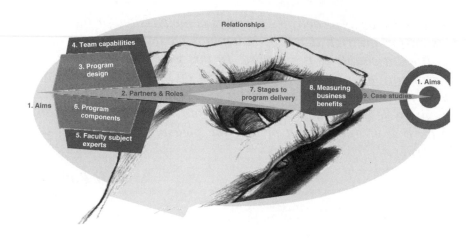

Customized programs are by definition unique interventions. Their anchor is their aim. Clarity on this at the start of all discussions is incredibly valuable. And yet, aims have a habit of changing. Be prepared for aims to evolve as you canvas opinion during the design phase and as potential designs are explored and detailed. Sometimes it is better to scale back the aim in order to have a better chance of delivering the quantifiable desired benefits. At other times you may need to amplify the aim to secure more sustainable development.

Underpinning the aim is the partnership between the client, the development team and the delivering faculty. Each must play their unique role within a relationship of transparency that inculcates trust.

To this end, program design is a fundamental activity. The final design must be clear yet flexible, focused on the development purpose yet able to incorporate new subjects or experiences in the light of evolution within the corporate and/or its environment.

To ensure this, listen to views from the diverse parts of the commissioning organization. Impartially gather the ideas of those from within the population earmarked for development. Take the time to capture the expectations of major individual stakeholders, of those who support and those who oppose the initiative. These include not only possible participants but also executives more senior and less senior than those of the target population – the managers and "n+1" of possible participants as well as individuals reporting into the development cadre. The views of the internal learning and development team are also critical. Not only do they hold the wider perspective on the totality of development activity within the organization, they are also the ones who will ultimately have to account for the value delivered by "your" specific development program. And because a corporate never stays the same, regular re-design together with continuous tucks and adjustments should be a feature of all customized programs to ensure program aims remain on-track.

Assembling the right delivery team is key to the success of transformational programs. Commissioning parties and participants have to trust the expertise of those who will manage, deliver and oversee the program. Trust is notoriously difficult to secure. The credibility of individual team members must be established through the expertise with which each fulfills their role, their visible collaboration within the collective and their personal approachability. By association, credibility can thus accumulate to the team as a whole. Together the delivery team must create a safe zone for participants to explore new knowledge and to explore themselves as principal actors, managers and leaders in the application of that new thinking.

Within the above, the engagement of passionate subject experts, of faculty, is critical and difficult. Take time to appeal to faculty as individuals. Try to understand what elements of the client, the client's environment, the program itself and/or the positioning of their subject would most appeal to them as professionals. Work with them, stepping into the shoes of the program participants, to make their subject a living activity, pragmatic and practicable.

Of infinitely more value than a pure educational activity, customized programs serve to develop executives as a whole, not just cognitively. Even when the aim of a program emphasizes the acquisition of knowledge more than leadership (behavioral) development, the ultimate purpose of any customized program is to raise the professionalism of the target population. For that to be attained, participants have to commit to doing things differently and in some cases to doing different things. To this end, the process of learning stands apart from the content of learning. How sessions within programs build into each other and how participants are accompanied in their assimilation of the material is as important, some would say more important, than the content itself. Without relevant content, the program will feel empty. Without an effective process, and the collection of program components that contribute to this, the program will be little more than an intellectual exercise.

Whilst the above may seem like separate disciplines, the creation of customized development programs is a joined-up affair. Seven distinct steps, from how you prepare to win a commission to how you measure benefits derived, provide clear logic and sequence.

Professionalism demands regular and final evaluation of "business benefits" ensuing from the program. Corporates invest in the development of their talent in order that they, the talent, may deliver greater results, individually and collectively. Though increasingly used as a retention tool by leading organizations, "executive development" is an investment, in a sense no different to any other, which deserves to be called to account for the value it returns to the investing organization.

Having said all of the above, the life-blood of all customized programs is the multiplicity of relationships – inside of the delivery organization, between the delivery organization and the commissioning client, and with the individual participants who experience the program. Within the complexity of these dynamic relational networks and as the customization process unfolds, it is good to remember that participants are the focus of the intervention. Individual participant relationships are therefore the bedrock of continuous customization. Feedback in this context is immediate, but often also reasoned. Welcome it even as you professionally test it. Whilst upholding confidentiality, share its key themes with the prime program sponsor to avoid misunderstanding and to test materiality. Use it to adjust and re-adjust the program to the changing environment of the commissioning corporate, not least as represented by the collective of participants in-the-delivery-moment.

With the ongoing dialogue and partnership exchanges afforded by such relationships, customized programs can become a transformational corporate capability that spurs continuous corporate development.

Through this relational, client-centric, focused and flexible approach to individual and cadre development, corporates can harness their executives for the leadership task, equip them to forge the future and empower them to address today's challenges – sustainably.

To be continued! Cora Lynn Heimer Rathbone.

Acknowledgments

1. Unless otherwise specified, all quotes are from Cranfield School of Management Faculty.

Executive summary

1. The terms "program(s)" and "intervention(s) are used interchangeably, and so too are the terms "corporates," "organizations," and "companies".

Introduction

1. Though most business schools offer corporates the full suite of possible interventions that include dedicated research projects, open programs, accredited programs such as MBAs, EMBAs, DBAs and PhDs, assessment/development centers and psychometric evaluations, this book dedicates itself exclusively to six corporates' development journeys though the vehicle of customized programs/interventions.
2. Tony Russell, Director of Senior Executive Development, L'Oréal Group; August 2009.

Chapter 1: Program aims

1. Like looking in a mirror in the morning and being shocked by what we see …
2. Key question: What tools have you used in which specific situations and what resulted from that?
3. Explored further in Chapter 8.
4. EDF participants included experts, managers, senior managers, "heads of …" and "directors of …"
5. Stewart Milne Group participants included board directors, directors, senior managers, middle managers, and team leaders.

6. BNFL participants included board directors, directors, senior managers, middle managers.
7. Oracle participants were directors and senior directors.

Chapter 2: Partners and roles

1. For example, "Shall we share the program such that you do Module 1 and we'll do Module 2?"
2. For example, "How might we share Module 3?"
3. For example, "To tie it all together, would you oversee the application of learning across all modules and manage the program platform? We could then oversee the program storyline and end-of session syntheses across the program as a whole."
4. Cooperation between competitors such as Oracle working with SAP or HP to fulfill a client requirement. For further reading: *Co-opetition* by Barry J. Nalebuff and Adam M. Brandenburger (1996, New York: Doubleday).

Chapter 5: Faculty – subject experts

1. Though most business schools pay their internal faculty (as well as external associates) to deliver on corporate programs, some do not. For these rare business schools, the expectation is that academic faculty must teach a minimum number of hours per annum. It is their choice, in discussion with their head of department, how they distribute those hours between MBA and executive program teaching.
2. Spony Profile Model – a 360° development tool that maps an individual's work values and communication style against established dilemmas that differentiate between national cultures in order to anchor discussions of what that individual's behavior conveys in terms of consistency with both their own values and appropriateness given corporate and national expectations.
3. This is crucially anchored from the start on the development partner's understanding of what the client organization means by "the subject in question" such that the faculty subject expert, with external-to-the-corporate perspectives, builds his/her contribution upon the same.

Chapter 7: Stages to program delivery

1. Dr Joe Jaina, Cranfield School of Management.
2. RFP = Request for proposal; whether formal or informal.

3. For example, the relevant business units and the functions.
4. For example, where several specialist organizations have to work in a synchronized, seamless manner to deliver a combined result such as a new airport terminal.

Chapter 8: Measuring business benefits

1. Chris Edwards and Rob Lambert:

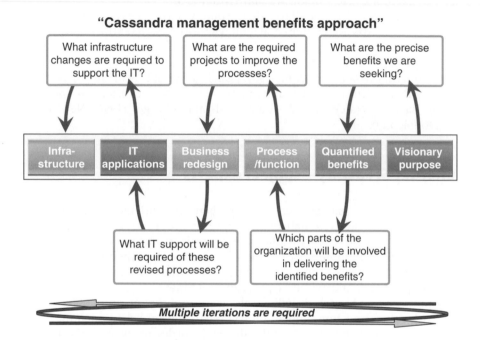

"Cassandra management benefits approach"

| What infrastructure changes are required to support the IT? | What are the required projects to improve the processes? | What are the precise benefits we are seeking? |

| Infra-structure | IT applications | Business redesign | Process /function | Quantified benefits | Visionary purpose |

What IT support will be required of these revised processes?

Which parts of the organization will be involved in delivering the identified benefits?

Multiple iterations are required

Chapter 9: Corporate journeys

1. A preferred style is to partner the teaching faculty through all of the session, continuously. As program director, this enables us to provide the red thread between sessions, together with executive coaching to all participants and support and feedback to faculty. As such the program director is uniquely placed to capture all discussions and identify key themes running through the hierarchy and the different populations. Within the bounds of confidentiality, the overall program director is thus able to present key issues to the corporate for their internal follow-through. The value added by this by-product should not be underestimated.
2. Whatever our style, the process of leadership echoes the three states of human existence, how we *think, take action*, and *relate*. Leaders set

destinations (where they want to get to and why), align resources (even if that is only their own time) and engage others (even if that is only their whole self). Provocatively, a "leader" who only aligns resources and engages others is a "manager", delivering to someone else's destination; a "leader" who only sets designations and engages others risks delusion, promising much but delivering little; a "leader" who only sets destinations and aligns resources may tend towards dictatorship.

3. A partnership for the purposes of this bid between URS (Washington Group), AMEC and Areva.
4. Merit good: a product or service that is essential to social/human civilization as we know it today, to which every individual arguably has a human right (merit).
5. Six distinct researched organizational structures (configurations) are emerging from the resource-based view of the firm that support different styles of corporate leadership, emphasize different organizational priorities and support different degrees of control.
6. "Cora Lynn: you and I don't have the same understanding of 'value'!"
7. See Note 2, Chapter 5.
8. Key tools that excluding process consulting, originated from Cranfield research and formed part of the program's integrated change process.
9. This acquisition strategy is approved in the United States, still in the process of approval by the EC at time of writing.
10. The front runners: pelaton in French refers to the leading group in a bicycle race.
11. As in the Olympic pentathlon, corporates that wish to be successful in innovation need to be good at all five activities explored within the "Innovation Pentathlon" (a management framework developed at Cranfield by Keith Goffin and Richard Mitchell to teach the subject of Innovation).